Lyn

Parenting for Tomorrow

with my very best wishes
Hope you enjoy reading this
book

7/08

Parenting for Tomorrow

A Results-Oriented Approach
to Preparing Your Child
for Tomorrow's World

John Samuel

VANTAGE PRESS
New York

Cover design by Polly McQuillen

FIRST EDITION

Published by Vantage Press, Inc.
419 Park Ave. South, New York, NY 10016

Manufactured in the United States of America
ISBN: 978-0-533-15839-3

Library of Congress Catalog Card No.: 2007904684

0 9 8 7 6 5 4 3 2 1

To my granddaughter, Jizan, for typing and re-typing the drafts of this publication and who has been a tower of support and inspiration to me in more ways than she'll ever know; to all of our dedicated therapists at Family and Consulting Services, Inc., and those whose lives have been transformed through their efforts; and to everyone whose loyalty and support have made our accomplishments possible throughout the years. My best wishes to you all!

Contents

Foreword

The values we teach our children are the best form of protection from the overwhelming number of challenges they'll face in these rapidly changing times. But, there's a great sense of helplessness on the part of us, parents, in teaching such values to kids, who themselves feel overwhelmed with conflicts of their own—often from external forces—as they run counter to the very principles and standards we'd like them to assimilate.

The result? Defiance, disrespect, and erosion of parental authority!

But there's hope and *Parenting for Tomorrow* offers an array of adaptable tools—and information—aimed at increasing both the awareness and understanding of your children's needs, plus practical methods for helping you reestablish confidence and your own authority.

I've known John Samuel, the author, for many years as a friend and colleague. His passion for helping families through difficult times is what he enjoys most and *Parenting for Tomorrow* is an extension of his ongoing work.

Careful application of its principles will help modify your parenting approach in these difficult times and hopefully improve your parenting skills overall.

—Joseph Ewa, M.D.
Child Psychiatrist

Preface

Although I'm familiar with numerous child development theories and the positive role parents can play in teaching values that shape their children's lives, much of what I've written in *Parenting for Tomorrow* is anecdotal based on my own experiences working with parents and their children during the last thirty-five years.

My first experience came serendipitously while teaching in London, England, where I frequently met with parents to discuss academic progress and behavioral issues.

My first job as family counselor here in the United States—which included home visits—also provided an opportunity to meet with many families in a home environment as opposed to working in an office setting.

Those many years of service overall, which include my former role as program director for two established social service agencies here in New York, and currently, as CEO for Family and Consulting Services, Inc., have provided me with a wealth of knowledge and experience, much of which I'm about to share with you here.

The material itself is based on a collection of my own writings, articles taken from *KIDS FOCUS,* a monthly publication of Family and Consulting Services, Inc., published since 1994 in which I acknowledge and applaud the efforts of parents who instill in their children core values aimed at guiding them along a positive path while encouraging the use of new and different approaches aimed at emboldening and empowering them to lead successful lives in tomorrow's world.

Also highlighted are: grandparenting issues, such as selfless-ness and the untold number of sacrifices they make caring for their grandchildren!

An entire section on informal education or role modeling is also included. This often holds the key to a child's development and his/her own understanding of the world.

In no way are they intended to teach you how to parent your child, however, but rather to enhance and strengthen your own ex-isting skills. Teaching these skills is especially difficult since there are no known, universal formulas or generally accepted standard for doing so. "It's often the quality of our understanding, often the intuitive understanding of a parent who is in intimate rapport with her child that provides the right method at critical moments."

The motivation for the book itself comes from an impelling urge to invest continuously in my immediate clientele while em-powering a much wider audience both at home and elsewhere and I do hope that it'll work well for you whether you live in Brooklyn, New York; London, England; OR in the most remote regions of Sub-Saharan Africa.

Acknowledgments

To the many wonderful people whose support over the years has helped—directly or indirectly—to make *Parenting for Tomorrow* what it is.

Particular thanks goes, to Dr. Quinton Wilkes, Psychologist/Consultant, whose unwavering support has been a source of inspiration to me over many, many years; to Joseph Ewa, MD, Psychiatrist, for his encouragement during earlier times; to Densley Sylvan, a longtime friend, and the first to suggest that I write a book relating to my line of work and its benefits to the community.

Special thanks also, to a few extraordinary people who'd rather remain nameless, but who have done their best behind the scenes whenever I needed their support.

I just want to take this opportunity to thank you all.

How to Use This Book

Parenting for Tomorrow is composed of six parts. You may begin with sections or topics of particular importance to you, even jump toward the very end and begin with "THINGS YOU NEED TO KNOW." Or, read from beginning to end. Your choice! But I wrote the book in such a way that you can turn to any section or chapter or start reading in any order you wish and never feel that you've missed out on anything.

On the "he/she?" dilemma that all writers face: With the awkwardness of their frequent use stepping in I was forced to vary them in many places—sometimes "he," sometimes "she." Needless to say, I mean every child, regardless of gender.

Parenting for Tomorrow

Part I

Relationship Building and Effective Communication

- Successful Parenting in a World of Change
- Build a Strong Foundation First
- Example of Good Moral Values
- Positive Role Modeling That Works

One

Successful Parenting in a World of Change

Around two and a half years ago I ran into an angry sixty-five-year-old woman desperately attempting to withdraw some cash from an ATM machine at a bank in downtown Brooklyn, New York. It was a few days before Christmas with scores of other frantic shoppers also waiting in line.

I recall our brief encounter quite vividly since she, in so many ways, reminded me of a dear aunt of mine with whom I'd had lots of fun, particularly during my adolescence years. We spoke for around fifteen minutes and toward the end of a reasonably upbeat conversation she said: "But Sir, sometimes I feel like living in a fishing boat somewhere. Life on land has become too complicated for me."

Sentiments like these are being echoed everywhere nowadays and chances are you too, share that feeling at times. If you do you're not alone. Times have really changed. I for one grew up in a world that for the most part doesn't exist anymore.

There are those who'll even admit that given the frenetic pace of things the person they once were has completely disappeared. Thankfully this isn't my experience but it has become quite a challenge to navigate in today's society amidst the madness and stresses of modern day living and the many influences of modern life.

The challenges faced by our young boys and girls are by far

more insurmountable, however, with peer pressure, violence, and despair on the one hand, substance abuse and addiction on the other, as well as other challenges which seemingly are a foretaste of what life might be like having to live in tomorrow's world.

Here's where we as parents come to the fore and the difficulty of the task is no excuse for avoiding it! Not only doing your duty in fact, but looking for more to do, and finding it!

So Where Do You Begin?

I personally believe that we must return to strong family values as a first step—setting the stage if you like, unlike "permissive parenting" in the nineteen sixties that has produced a generation of adults, who've broken every conceivable record in areas such as drug abuse, family instability among others.

In many ways, on becoming adults, they weren't different people than they were as children, merely "older children" whose needs evolved rather than changed. And whatever happens in your kids' lives today will also return later in their own lifetime with astounding accuracy!

As parents we're their strongest influence and the oasis for their moral and spiritual development. But so much has been lost. Before fast food and television (and more recently, the Internet), families actually sat down at the table and ate together. Grandparents were central to all of this. The entire community in fact, played its part in raising a child and research has shown enormous benefits to this seemingly forgotten and overlooked tradition.

So what do you wish for that'll bring not just instant delight, etc., but lasting positive results for those you love so dearly? This is a personal question. But bear in mind, that if you ask for success and prepare for failure, failure will be the outcome—you'll get only the outcome you've prepared for.

But the fact that you've bought this book suggests one thing:

4

that you are without doubt, thoroughly invested in the growth, development and welfare of your child. It was written for you if you are:

- A single mom often having to do two or three jobs just to make ends meet
- An absentee dad
- An ostracized dad, broken and confused!
- A married couple with overscheduled lifestyles!
- Widowed, struggling to cope with separation or loss!
- A grandparent. Thankfully you're actively parenting again!

It's also aimed at community members as a whole including those with no children of their own.

Hopefully, you will use it as an instrument therefore, to reach all of your loved ones in ways that'll help them make the right choices today—one choice at a time—so that they'll be better prepared for the joyous and fulfilling lives they deserve in tomorrow's world.

Two
Build a Strong Foundation First

As parents, we all have one thing in common: we want our children to grow up to be purposeful and responsible citizens that everyone loves and respects. We want them to learn to feel, think and act with respect not only for themselves but also with respect for others.

Importantly, we conscientiously attempt to provide our children with avenues to explore academically; something to "shoot" for; walking the high road if you like, full of great expectations, as opposed to taking the low road that'll diminish the effectiveness of their lives.

Of course, in spite of our best efforts, there's no foolproof way to getting everything right when it comes to raising children. One way to ensure that they meet some or all of your expectations, however, is by helping them develop good character traits, building a strong foundation if you like, that'll help them recognize the correlation between value-based living and their own long-term happiness.

It won't always be easy and your approach may be directly influenced, even dictated by your own circumstances.

A few years ago I spoke on this very subject at a family life conference where it was widely acknowledged that the family unit as we once knew it had fundamentally changed. During a question and answer session, a thirty-seven-year-old man stood up and said: "My sister, a young mother of three, is now forced to raise three kids with little or no support through no fault of hers!" He recounted many harrowing stories and I was deeply moved not just by his care and concern, but by his courage and desire to help her rise above her difficulties.

One week later I met with his sister, a selfless mom who worked herself almost to a fault trying to raise those kids the best way she knew how in spite of her own challenging circumstances. She had many sad stories to tell but told them so gracefully that I'll always remember her with admiration and respect.

There are so many sad stories everywhere!

Every day on the radio, television, in the newspapers and magazines, as well as talking with teachers, even with parents and children alike, everyone acknowledges that there is a problem, that our children's needs aren't being met mentally, physically or spiritually.

As you listen to many of the kids themselves you can't help but get a sense of helplessness and hopelessness with regard to their future; their fears of being incarcerated or passing on their bleak childhood to their offspring. And depending on where they live, their fears of being killed by age twenty—the life expectancy of children living in a certain deprived neighborhoods according to new research.

Sadly, children even as young as three, sometimes younger, are being abandoned by their parents to the care of strangers.

Families in turmoil, in particular, often overlook the needs and responsibilities of teaching values to their children. This is sad since each and every child is born with the potential to achieve greatness. Modeled and nurtured they can be directed along the path to their own fulfillment and good fortune.

Regardless of your own circumstances, parenting is for life, however. And with many years of parenting ahead of you now is the time to embrace the many challenges that come with the task.

You may be forced to adapt or change certain methodologies

based on your own circumstances. But there's no excuse for doing nothing.

It all begins with you, and the best way to make a really good start is by making your relationship with your kids as good as it can get, and instilling strong discipline and self-management values as a first step.

Get into the habit of talking with them every day. Build a close relationship with them. Not only will this make it easier for them to come to you when they need help, it'll also help you become more sensitive to their needs.

Building a strong parent-child relationship will also help you see the strengths in what you may have otherwise perceived and their weaknesses and help you celebrate them exactly as they are.

Building a strong family relationship as a whole cannot be over-emphasized. We'll be discussing more on the subject shortly, and throughout the book.

Three
Example of Good Moral Values

A TV station in our local area recently covered in glowing terms, a news item relating to the honorable deeds of two young students who, having found a pocketbook containing $500 made the decision to return it to its rightful owner, who in turn, thanked and gave them $1.00 each for their "thoughtfulness and honesty."

While it was refreshing to hear of such noble acts, though, it was also of great interest to note that other boys in the same school when asked what would they have done with such a find, replied unanimously, "We'd keep it all!"

But what captured my attention above all else, was the manner in which the community responded to the news. Within days of the story being reported, many ordinary residents came together, raised enough money and bought each boy a bicycle to say nothing of the number of compliments, and goodwill gestures made toward the parents of these two young men—sending a clear message on the importance of honesty, and that good deeds are often rewarded.

Good moral values do not occur by chance. And now, more than ever, is there a need to help your kids learn these most important lessons of all.

Apart from unconditional love—an instinctive thing which generally comes naturally—values and character development are two of the first things every parent should lavish on his or her child. In fact, they're two of the greatest gifts you can give.

While children may grow up and undoubtedly develop values of their own, values different from ours, they'll have more autonomy, independence, and confidence and will be happier as a result of having developed values-oriented behavior from home, especially at an early age.

Summary

As with every other institution, the institution of family needs its own value system, its own set of family values designed to help children make good choices; one that teaches them to accept responsibility for their own actions rather than blame their mistakes or misfortune on luck or on someone else; a moral system for practicing good moral behavior overall, one that's inherently right, that'll help rather than hurt others.

It is important therefore, that you, like every other parent reading this, make a conscious decision to develop your own system.

Four
Positive Role Modeling That Works

Is it enough in today's challenging world to just love our kids? No! It's our job to also teach them character values that'll lead to a balanced life experience and the many good fortunes that such experience often brings. The best way to do so is through example, being positive role models to them.

As parents, we have far more influence in our children's lives than we probably realize. In their eyes we're the most important people in the world. Their teacher! Their mentor! Their guide! Not only are our habits, beliefs, and behaviors reflected in what they do—or say, more often than not they believe sincerely that everything we say and do is true and the way to behave.

Thus, if you want your children to be on time, then you need to be on time. If you want them to be healthy and fit, you need to be healthy and fit. If you want them to be honest, you need to be honest, and so on.

Quite often we all wish that our children would simply do what we say not necessarily what we do. This is not how a child's mind works. Children model what they see. While they often ignore, even disbelieve—or appear to disbelieve—much of what we say, they'll always believe what we do. You must therefore be the best role model you can be. True, it is hard work, but it doesn't work any other way.

Role Modeling—Negative or Positive

The term role model on its own usually implies positive role model. This, however, isn't quite true. There's also negative role modeling. Example of a positive role model is someone who carries out an exemplary role, a role which signifies values, ways of thinking and acting generally considered positive in that role and/or in the wider society. A woman professor for instance, can be seen as a role model for other women on the strength of her furthering of the profile of women in academia. She may also be seen as a role model for aspiring academics, regardless of gender on the strength of her academic achievements and/or dedication to her chosen discipline.

QUESTION: How positive a role model are you?

In a recent online survey, nearly half of all young women respondents looked to their mothers as their role model. In another, 42 percent of 750 teens named a relative. In a third survey, 46 percent of teens said their role model was a family member.

A role model needs to be "real"; someone who lives by the highest code of conduct possible, cemented with integrity, impartiality, and honesty; someone who children can learn from throughout their formative years in particular. It is at this stage that their understanding of authority and rules of behavior are formed.

You're not their hero by the way. Athletes and movie stars are. You're their role model and as a positive role model, one of your biggest responsibilities and challenges is how you control what they are exposed to. When born, children are much like a new computer eager to store and process mass quantities of data and information. Their undeveloped mind, however, will make no distinction between the real and the unreal. If they see it done, they'll most probably want to try it themselves. Here's where parental censorship is so critical.

How well you control what they see on television for instance, will go a long way toward how they develop behaviorally.

There are many other ways to help your child in the character development process and the following tips will help.

- Be a strong and positive parent at all times
- Love and value your family
- Lead by example. How you talk in your kid's presence for instance will determine the language they'll use
- Set clear and reasonable boundaries and be consistent in keeping them. Being a parent isn't about saying yes all of the time
- Share your values and demonstrate why they are critical to their upbringing
- Demonstrate self-respect and self-esteem
- Respect others and take time to listen
- Value their independence
- Show sincere interest and get involved in their school activities. Volunteer for their school or community events if you can. Go to their little league games, their piano recitals
- Tell them you are interested in what goes on in their lives
- Show that you love them by spending time with them. Plan ahead for special trips to the zoo or take them to a movie they want to see. A walk around the neighborhood is OK too. Also, enjoy spontaneous activities such as going out for an ice cream. And be sure to tell them how much you enjoy being with them
- Find activities the entire family can do without the TV or without spending money unnecessarily. Play a game, read, build or bake something
- Teach them the spirit of giving
- Teach them how to work with their hands and learn to create something they can be proud of
- Teach them the importance of finishing a job they started
- Give each child specific responsibilities at home, such as

setting the table or walking the dog. It'll help develop a sense of teamwork and accomplishment
- Share with them how you set your own goals and how you plan to meet those goals
- Share success and failure stories not just success. They need to understand that they'll experience both. They need to also understand that struggles are a normal part of life. Let them know that failures are OK and that they can be used as learning experiences and as a springboard to success

Summary

The building block of everything our kids have is family, the people who ground them. And how we live our lives will surely structure their growth.

Take time therefore, to listen to your kids. Their number one complaint is that we do not listen to them or listen enough. Set up a time to talk, a special moment spent together that'll enable them to open up, tell you how their day went, what they liked, what they learned, what was not so good. Create a safe place and time for bonding and keep it going for as many years as you can. (Even at age sixteen, or older, they may still want those special moments to talk with you—alone!)

Show empathy and the kinds of sensitivity that you want them to mirror. Instead of the normal parental tendencies of directing, managing and interrogating, try to really hear what they say and make your own listening and caring obvious.

We all have a stake in helping our kids create a better world and here's where strong, moral leadership really counts! Do the best you can and expect the best.

Part II

Fundamentals of Positive Behavior

- Building a Healthy Self-esteem
- Social Skills—a Prerequisite for Upward Mobility
- Consistent Discipline and Self-management
- Positive Self-talk and How It Can Help Your Child's Future

Five
Building a Healthy Self-esteem

As an adolescent, or teenager, your child could spend much of his or her life losing friends and missing out on so many of the good things in life. As an adult he/she may end up spending thousands of dollars in therapy sessions complaining about poor relationships and even more on anti-depressants to help cope with ruined friendships, never knowing why.

Why? Lack of a healthy self-esteem! Self-esteem is a major key to success in everyone's life. It's all about how we feel about ourselves: too fat; too skinny; too short; too tall; too young; too old; too weak; too slow; too frizzy, too straight, too curly, bald; small teeth; big teeth; crooked teeth; living in a dirty, rundown home/neighborhood; poor physical appearance.

Yes, who we believe we are forms the basis or sets the tone if you like, for everything we'll do and experience and our behavior clearly reflects those feelings or beliefs.

For more than 100 years, specialists and educators have disagreed on much of the precise nature and development of self-esteem. They nevertheless, generally agree that its foundation is laid early in life—by parents and adults who are important to a child—even as early as infancy, in response to his/her cries and smiles.

Needless to say, this changes as they grow older when their self-esteem, high or low, is based largely on their perceptions of how they are judged and the extent to which they believe they are valued.

Self-esteem is an ever flowing reflection of what we think about ourselves. It also has its high and low moments depending on what is happening at any given time. When in its low state, even the best forms of praises showered on us by others—though they may make us feel a little better for a while—are short-lived.

In my line of work, I witness some of those difficulties first hand—from ten-year-olds looking for a place to belong, to successful, well-admired, middle income earners, who, in spite of their many outer "successes," continue to feel empty, unfulfilled, and in some cases, even unworthy of their accomplishments. And I often ask myself what good is any kind of success in life if you can't completely enjoy it?

Outer successes by themselves won't guarantee your child's happiness either. A healthy self-esteem, on the other hand, can.

And Can You Help?

Yes! As a parent, you, more than anyone else can—by your words and actions more than anything else; by infusing positive attitudes designed to alter your child's moment by moment internal thought processes and replacing them with positive self-esteem building patterns. Let's call it a set of behavior modification exercises for want of a simpler term.

It isn't particularly difficult. In fact, most parents do it without even realizing it.

Begin by Making Them Feel Special and Appreciated

Set aside "special time" alone with each child. If he/she is pretty young, it'll be helpful to say, "When I read to you or play with you, I won't even answer the phone if it rings." Also, during these special moments, focus on things he/she enjoys doing.

Among other things, it'll provide an opportunity to relax and display his/her strengths.

Research indicates that one of the contributing factors to a child's resiliency and high self-esteem is the presence of at least one adult who'll help that child feel special and appreciated; an adult who won't ignore her problems, but one who'll focus on her strengths.

Give her the best of you—everyday; make time for fun, time to laugh, and nothing but time. It may seem difficult to a busy parent, yes. Yet, it's far less difficult than solving problems caused by her low self-esteem later in life!

Action is also necessary for high self-esteem to take hold and blossom. Helping them develop problem-solving and decision-making skills is a good way in which it can be fostered.

For example, if your child is having difficulty with a friend, you may ask him/her to think about a couple of ways through which they can resolve the situation. Don't worry if he/she can't think of an immediate solution. It may take a little while. Also, try role playing situations to help demonstrate the steps involved.

Assigning chores to children at an early age is also a great way to help instill self-discipline and a sense of responsibility.

Provide Opportunities to Help

Children seem to have an inborn need to help others. Providing opportunities so they can fulfill that need is a positive step in nurturing their "reservoir of competence." Getting them involved in charitable work is one possible way to do so.

Offer Them Choices

Ask, for example, if he/she would like to be reminded to get ready for bed five or ten minutes before bedtime. A simple choice, but one that'll help lay the foundation for the nurturing of his/her decision-making capabilities, even at this early stage.

Highlight Their Strengths

Unfortunately, many youngsters view themselves in a negative light. Make a list of their areas of strength and find ways to reinforce and display them. If he or she is into art, for instance, display his/her artwork.

Things to Avoid:

1. Avoid accusatory or judgmental comments

Many children do try hard and still have difficulty. Say instead, "We'll figure out a different or a better way to help you," an approach framed in more positive terms and one that'll also enhance their problem-solving skills.

Do not compare siblings. This is important. Highlight the strengths of every child in the family.

And Here Are a Few Facts:

1. As they grow, children become increasingly sensitive to the evaluations of their peers.
2. As they develop stronger ties with their peers—in school or around the neighborhood—they may begin to evaluate themselves differently from the way they were taught at home.
3. Children often feel self-confident and accepted at home, not necessarily so, elsewhere. They may also feel accepted and liked one moment and different the next.
4. A child's sense of self-worth deepens when adults re-

spond to his/her interests with appreciation rather than just praise.

5. The more things they're good at and the more challenging goals they attain, the more opportunities they'll have to feel good about themselves.

6. Stereotyping, prejudice, and discrimination are contributory factors to low self-esteem.

7. Self-esteem is also related to children's feelings of belonging to a group and being able to adequately function in that group.

8. Poor health, low energy, and an out of shape, unattractive body is a recipe for low-self esteem. Few children are aware of the impact of their health on other areas of their lives.

9. Children maintain a healthier self-esteem when assisted in coping with defeats, rather than emphasizing constant successes and triumphs. Excessive praise and flattery are often counter-productive. They also raise doubts in their minds. Even at a tender age children can see through flattery and may even dismiss an adult who heaps on praise, as a feeble source of support and one who isn't believable.

Conclusion

All of the above areas discussed intertwine and determine how high or low a child's self-image or self-esteem will be at any point in time! As their old self-defeating beliefs wither away and new ones blossom, it will become natural for them to take themselves less seriously which will be reflected in everything they do.

If they continue to experience difficulty stripping away those old self-esteem-destroying patterns, and negative beliefs about themselves, however, be empathetic and say, "I understand that you continue to have difficulties," and then, cast the difficulty as a problem to be solved and involve him/her in thinking about a possible solution.

Six

Social Skills—A Prerequisite for Upward Mobility

One skill that'll mean as much to your child's success and happiness in life as any other will be his or her ability to get along well with others.

It has made fortunes for thousands of men and women all over the world, many from humble beginnings such as Henry Ford, among others.

Your child may be the smartest kid around, have the best resume, be best looking, dressed in the finest clothes . . .

But those things won't matter much or matter at all when it comes to social interactions and maintaining meaningful or lasting relationships. Often it's not what you know or how much you have, as much as, who you happen to know.

Rooted in every field of knowledge are various lessons that demonstrate and validate certain principles essential to our individual and collective well-being. Social interaction is one of those. It's a simple mental training that'll provide your child with the ability to do and say the things that'll make him as influential as he may want to be, and become so well-liked that people will feel drawn to him as if by a magnet.

Self-confidence itself is directly related to social skills and social interaction. Yet many kids have very little idea how to interact appropriately, even with their classmates or their peers. In fact, they often lack the social skills needed to perform the most basic cooperative tasks. Lack of social skills is also among the biggest contributing factors to lack of academic success in many teens, studies have revealed.

With something that'll touch so many aspects of their lives it is therefore of great importance that they learn it well. In fact, it can be taught in the same way as any academic skill and coming up are a number of tips that you may freely use to help guide them should you need to.

But before we begin, let's take a look at a few social situations some of which, because of just one thing you may have said or done—or didn't do—may have led to awkward moments or people treating you not as well as you would have expected them to; or where things didn't work out well for you. Worse, you had no idea why.

1. Do you shake inside when meeting new people or during job interviews?
2. Do you feel invisible at social gatherings and do you wish you weren't there at all?
3. Is meeting new people about as much fun as meeting with family members or other people with whom you are familiar?
4. Do people feel at ease with you socially or do they attempt to shy away from you?
5. Do your co-workers "forget" to invite you out with the "gang?" And do you not really care that they don't?
6. Do people often get angry with you for no apparent reason?
7. How many awkward dates have you been on where you just couldn't connect with the other person, regardless of how hard you tried?

Your answers may be of little significance right now, yet these and hundreds of other social situations may cost your child dearly during his lifetime. Fortunately it doesn't have to be this way and here are a few tips that can help make a difference:

1. Begin by discussing the need for social skills, the need for getting on well with others

Help him understand why these skills are so important. You may want to have him recall any problems he may have experienced at school, at church or in any social groups while relating to others. Then point out that most of these problems may have been brought about as a result of poor "social skills," sometimes referred to as "people skills."

Share with him that even adults need to work on their social skills from time to time!

2. Select a social skill

Have him brainstorm a list of social skills to work on for, let's say, the next six weeks then have him decide which ones he'd like to work on first. Offer a few suggestions yourself to get him started.

3. Teaching the skill

This step is not as obvious as it might seem but it's not enough to say, "Be nice!" You have to help him identify exactly what he needs to do and say in order to "Be nice."

4. Practice the skill

Once you both agree to a particular skill for a given time, offer him the chance to practice that skill. It's always best to focus on one skill at a time.

Although far easier said than done, here are a few more ideas that may be helpful:

1. Encourage communication and interaction with other people. EXAMPLE: Take him to let's say, a building site and while there, ask if he'd like to ask the workers a question about their work. "What are you mixing in that bin?" for instance.
2. Role-play difficult social situations. Have him practice asking the teacher for an extension of time for a paper or talking with an employer on a job interview. You can play the teacher's or prospective employer's role and offer a feedback.
3. Encourage mature, topic-centered conversations:
    - "How was work today?" "And what did you do?"
    - "Did you do anything else?"
    - Talk about your own experiences in an awkward situation and ask what would he have done
    - When you disagree on a point (you occasionally will), encourage him to appropriately defend his point of view

4. Encourage him to join group conversations
5. Teach him the hidden rules of conversation
6. Teach him how best to enter a conversation when he's got something to say. If he attempts to dominate the conversation, explain that people often feel angry at those who talk out of turn or talk too much
7. Finally, teach him strategies such as:
    - Looking at other people's faces as they speak
    - Counting the number of times they speak
    - Learning the signals people make when they want to interrupt someone
    - Maintaining eye contact as they speak and devel-

oping body language so that they can keep the
floor and avoid interruptions

NOTE: Even though it wasn't possible to cover this huge
subject in greater details here—due to space constraints—hopefully it'll go a long way in contributing to your child's success and
happiness in life as it relates to his ability to get along well with
others. May he indeed become the most likable human being
alive!

Seven

Consistent Discipline and Self-management

Child discipline is an important parenting function and skill that all parents need to learn. It may take different forms depending on the age and maturity of the child. But discipline is essential and should begin even at the earliest stages of a child's development.

Research has shown that children who grow up with strong discipline and self-control are better able to balance their personal wants and needs against those of others. It's also one way to help develop their sense of self-worth and responsibility while at the same time, developing their sense of community.

The subject of discipline is often misunderstood, though, so it is important to have a clear understanding, of what it really is, and what it isn't.

First of all, discipline isn't synonymous with punishment such as hitting, spanking or the application of any kind of physical pain in response to undesirable behavior. While spanking for instance, may be used to directly control a child's behavior it does not teach how to change what he/she does.

Discipline on the other hand, is guidance; teaching; teaching right from wrong; how to respect the rights of others; which behaviors are acceptable and which are not.

Of equal importance, is helping your kids acquire self-management skills, and the main goal here should be to assist in the development of skills that they can use to control themselves: setting limits; impulse control, etc., and to take responsibility for their own behavior.

But the effective guidance of young children is a slow process, frustrating, at times unpleasant—for parents and children alike. It also requires nurturing parents with lots of patience and time and may also demand some important shifts in your own thinking bearing in mind that by their own developmental nature, young children are egocentric—they think only about their own needs; they also think about the present, the here and now. As they get older they'll learn to consider others and to think beyond the present.

A big part of the disciplinary process is getting to know your child well, at every phase of his/her development. Let us therefore, take a general look at their social developmental stages up to the age of eight with advice on how he/she may be treated at each stage. Pay particular attention if you are a first time mom.

1. Newborn to Eighteen Months—Learning to Trust

Cries for needs; uses senses to learn about the world; explores "who am I."

YOU: Give lots of attention; nurturance; respond quickly to cries; provide opportunities for exploring his/her world through taste, touch, etc. Help him/her feel that the world is a safe and good place where needs are met with loving care.

2. One Year to Mid-Twos—Learning Independence

Curious, messy, affectionate; like to do things "by myself"; shows emerging independence; bites; has temper tantrums; explores; starts to test limits; begins to talk, run and climb.

YOU: Show affection and respect; have lots of patience and a sense of humor; keep limits simple and consistent; avoid setting up power plays over food, sleep; offer choices; help balance independence with limits; try to reason, but do not expect miracles.

3. Mid-Twos to Four—Learning Identity

Cooperates; tries hard to please; learns new skills; talks a lot; has lots of energy and enjoys noise; develops likes and dislikes for food.

YOU: Again, show affection and respect; continue to set firm, consistent limits; laugh together, help them find answers to many of their own questions; discover things together.

4. Mid-Threes to Five—Still Learning Identity

Bold, quarrelsome, contrary, full of energy and zest for life; goes from independence to clinging; uses "naughty" words; tells bold stories that may sound untrue; has difficulty sharing or playing cooperatively; learns and develops new skills and abilities.

YOU: Have understanding and patience; provide outlets and opportunities for an outburst of energy and developing intellect; continue with firm, consistent rules and expectations; accept the testing of limits with a sense of humor; begin to use reason and logic.

5. Mid-Fours to Six

Becomes more cooperative with age; shows lots of energy, wiggling, and giggling; loves to talk about self; can do many things and loves to show off; has many new fears; still tells tales; may have interest in things that belong to others; shows interest in numbers and letters; begins to play cooperatively with others, but disagreements can easily occur.

YOU: Give affection, clear directions, and expectations; encourage the trying of new things; provide a variety of activities that allow him/her to learn by doing; let him/her participate in planning activities and doing small, helpful chores; provide opportunities to show off skills.

6. Mid-Fives to Eight—Learning to Be Productive

Fair minded; shows off; insists on following rules fairly, often to a fault; prefers friends of the same sex; makes and loses friends; likes special projects that seem useful, and grown-up; tests limits with determination.

YOU: Allow flexibility, affection, respect, and moments of undivided attention; set clear but reasonable limits; assign simple household duties with reminders; be fair and reasonable; provide opportunities to join organized activities without overscheduling; offer him/her opportunities to plan personal activities.

As they grow older, there will undoubtedly be other influences in their lives such as TV, the Internet, and their peers among others.

There's where a different set of disciplinary approaches may be required. The taking away of privileges from one child for instance; the application of timeout to another OR, making use of reward systems for rewarding good behavior!

By having laid a good foundation so far it should become by far easier to administer. But they must be applied with consistency.

Eight

How Positive Self-talk Can Impact Your Child's Future

What we say to ourselves every day is critical to our own development and well being. It's true, and if you think you do not talk to yourself, think again. We all do. This is known as self-talk, and more and more people are becoming aware of it and its impact. It influences our behavior; affects our confidence and self-esteem among other things, and can shape our emotions and behavior for good—or bad. Once that seed is planted in our subconscious it forces us to carry out whatever action is necessary to justify it.

Yet, most of us go about doing what we do unaware of how or how much we talk to ourselves, and the negative or positive impact such self-communication can have on our lives.

The Power of Positive Self-talk

If you believe that thoughts precede moods—and they do—then you will agree that unhappy thoughts for instance, can make us feel, and become unhappy. The opposite is also true and most successful people will agree that not only do they think happy thoughts—they frequently make happy, positive statements about themselves, to themselves.

In her book, *Confident Conversation,* Dr. Lillian Class, speech pathologist, author and one of the world's foremost author-

32

ities on communication and self-image provides a wonderful example of this.

"One of the most amazing clients I've ever had", says Dr. Class, "was a Texan businessman who told me that every morning after he woke up he'd look at himself in a mirror and, in his most positive, enthusiastic voice would say, 'Good morning, Wayne. It's so good to see you. We're going to have a terrific day! All kinds of terrific things are going to happen to us. We're going to have fun and make a lot of money today!' " According to Dr. Class, Wayne made millions.

Like positive self-talk, however, negative self-talk is also self-fulfilling and many of us become its victims at one point or another. In a recent study, psychiatrist Martin Seligman referred to it as "Learned Helplessness." It is destructive and often leads to low self-esteem, lack of confidence, even depression and consequently more negative or destructive self-talk—a vicious circle!

Positive self-talk, on the other hand, also referred to as "Learned Optimism," focuses on our strengths, resiliency, and other attributes conducive to making positive changes, hence the positive results.

Anecdotal and other studies also show a strong correlation between frequently used negative statements and poor academic performance and behavior among children, in particular. Interestingly, these same studies have found that in households with optimistic parents where positive statements are frequently made, their child's academic performance and behavior have shown greater promise overall.

Children are especially vulnerable to negative statements, so much so that these statements often become part of their own vocabulary. "I'm bad! I'm stupid! I'm never good at anything! No one really likes me! I can't!"

One of our former clients (now a really promising young man), has for many years been a victim of such negative comments to the point of hating himself and his experience mirrors many others with whom I've had the privilege of working over the years. Interestingly, Patrick (not his real name for reasons of confidentiality) now wears a near permanent smile thanks in part to his own willingness to overcome persistent negative thinking, the ability to rely on himself to change, and discovering his own creative power and potential.

Negative self-talk emanates from a number of sources. Chief among them are: lack of confidence and low self-esteem. If you're told repeatedly early in life for instance, that you're useless, a failure or worse, there's a good chance you'll eventually accept and believe you are, and act on that belief.

Deep inside, we also have what Don Miguel Ruis, author of *The Four Agreements* refers to as "an inner judge who is more critical than anybody you've ever met," someone who's unforgiving and lethal to our self-confidence and true potential!

Negative cultural influences and family styles also play a big part.

What Can You Do to Help Your Child Stay Positive?

First of all you'll need to create an environment based on love, kindness, respect, and strong moral values; clearly defined values such as trust, honesty, self-discipline; an environment where you can talk so the kids will listen and the other way round. That's step one.

Step two: Help build their self-esteem and confidence by feeding their minds with positive affirmations.

What this will do is begin a process of combating all negative thoughts, etc. stored in their subconscious—the negative things they may have told themselves over time without even realizing it—and start replacing those misguided negative messages with new, positive ones.

But affirmations will work only if they're honest about them and here are a few that might be helpful:

"I deserve to be happy!"
"I deserve to be loved!"
"I have the power to change my life!"
"I can choose happiness whenever I wish irrespective of the
    circumstance!"
"I am flexible and open to change in every aspect of my life!"
"I will act with confidence at all times!"

Encourage daily repetitions but urge them to develop their own.

Final Note: Most of what happens in our lives can be attributed to our thinking, the way we think about ourselves.

"Attitude" (Positive Attitude) is everything. It's what often makes the difference between those who succeed and those who don't.

Thus, as parent or guardian, you'll need to make that extra effort to consistently talk encouragingly to your child. These are among the best protection against negative influences, peer pressure and even the "culture of cruelty" faced by boys in particular, in the real world.

And even when things didn't go quite right, encourage them to say positive things such as: It wasn't as pleasant an experience as I'd expected but I can (and will) learn from it!

Part III

Fostering Self-reliance and Responsibility

- Defining and Setting Achievable Goals
- Maintaining Authority
- Education—The Key to a Really Great Future
- The Effects of Peer Pressure and How You Can Help

Nine
Defining and Setting Achievable Goals

Learning goal achievement strategies is essential in helping to shape your children's future. It'll help strengthen their resolve as they strive to become self-reliant productive citizens and lead productive lives.

Goals are a prelude to action and the milestones by which reality will find its way to their dreams. If they can communicate what they truly want, then they're more than halfway to achieving them as they'll be in direct alignment with what they value most.

Goal setting comes with its own rules, however. They MUST:

1. Decide and define what they want and establish a reason

Things that are significantly important to them. Vague descriptions of intent won't be good enough.

2. Make them realistic and achievable

I want to dance like Michael Jackson is a realistic goal! I want to fly like Superman isn't! Not every wish can be a goal. It must be within their power to accomplish.

3. Write them down

This is important! It'll help crystallize them in their minds while keeping them motivated and focused.

4. Establish a deadline

"I want to earn $200 to buy a new bicycle in six months."

5. Finding an objective or a mission will help

"I want to earn $1,000 to buy a computer for the school library" or "I want to raise $5,000 to help support AIDS victims in the community."

6. Create a plan of action

List what needs to be done to accomplish the task, and set a realistic plan for its achievement breaking each action down into step-by-step, doable increments.

7. Work the plan

Taking action will be the determining factor. Without action nothing will happen.

In order to succeed they may need your support both in terms of getting them started and helping them stay motivated. Here's what you can do:

1. To get started, help them brainstorm a little by asking questions such as:

    a. Can you think of something you'd like to accomplish in the next six months? Get a summer job, for instance?

b. If you could become anything you wanted, or accomplish anything you wanted in life, what would it be and what can you do to make that happen?

For each goal, let them describe in detail what they'll need to do in order to achieve it and lay out a plan for doing so—including deadlines.

As well as having long-term goals help set a few short-term ones—simple goals! Something to work towards; something to look forward to, and measure up to! Once accomplished help them set a few more, one goal at a time—so that they do not become overwhelmed.

They must also believe in what they do or they will lose the motivation or will to do it. Motivation can, in fact, melt on a single hot afternoon.

2. Set up some kind of a reward for each goal they achieve. Perhaps a special Sunday lunch for all of their friends; a cruise to the Statue of Liberty OR, a trip to Disney—anything!

IMPORTANT: goal setting is an important life skill and it'll be worth every moment of your time helping your child in the mastery of that skill. It will in turn, determine what lifestyle choices he or she ideally wants to pursue as it offers him/her an opportunity to literally identify and pursue his/her own dreams and desires, not just dream about them.

Ten

Maintaining Authority

Maintaining authority at home is a critical part of your child's upbringing and it is important that such authority be demonstrated and acknowledged.

Authority is the right to lead, govern or rule. Parents are endowed with such authority for the purpose of caring for the family and raising their children with a purpose for life. Yet many parents have mixed feelings about their own authority. Although they know that they are responsible for their children's upbringing, they fear that while maintaining authority, their own children may dislike, even hate them.

One mother with whom I've worked for sometime explained: "I almost lost control of my daughter, while hanging out with other youths in the neighborhood whose parents had no authority over them."

She subsequently admitted that she was equally responsible. "When you try to control your own child," she said, "she looks at you like, you know, you're old; you're boring; you're authoritarian, no one else is like that, you know!"

Yet (and this may surprise you) when your children—teens in particular—see you as being in charge, they pay a great deal of attention to what you say to them. They're the ones, in fact, who are likely to make good decisions about staying in school and coming home at a reasonable time. They know that all you want and expect of them is that they make good, responsible decisions. They also understand that negative consequences will follow if they don't.

After all, parents who maintain authority with their children do not bully them, lock them up or starve them to death. They simply try to help them understand the consequences of their own choices and follow through with negative consequences when they do not make the right ones.

This may take various forms and, of course, teens may see these measures as forms of punishment and may not appreciate their values—at least not now!

However, parents who maintain their ground and establish clear rules of conduct with consistent consequences are the ones who see their kids grow up to be grateful and appreciative adults in the end, for having maintained their ground.

Parental authority must always be matter-of-fact, with clear expectations: **"Bath time; play time; work time; dinner time; quiet time; bed time!"**

The tone of your voice, volume, pitch, and the purposefulness with which you say things is what will convey authority. If there is a hint of begging or pleading, all authority will be lost.

Of course as a parent you can easily fall into the "be nice" trap by asking her to do something in a voice that suggests, "Hey, I'm being nice, and I hope you will think so too."

More likely than not, what will happen here is that she'll suddenly seize control of the situation since you're obviously not in control.

You need to be firm in maintaining authority and there's nothing wrong with being firm as long as it is respectful and without cruelty.

When it is bedtime for instance, you need to let them know it's time for bed. You may ask, "Do you want to choose a story to read or do you want me to tell you one?" They know it is bedtime but that they will still have a reasonable choice to make on their own.

Unfortunately, many parents try to be authoritative without

having the know-how and often end up yelling and screaming when their children do not respond.

It's all about learning and it takes time.

Summary

1. Make your expectations clear. You need to establish a set of guidelines—or rules if you like—as a first step but bearing in mind that children learn more by examples than by precepts.
2. Talk like a parent who has self-control and believes in his/her own authority.
3. Help the child comply.
4. Be consistent, be patient.

Throughout the book you'll find various guidelines upon which you may base your own system. But whatever parenting rules you do lay down in the end, you'll need to explain the reason behind those rules and in a way that'll be clearly understood.

Once established, you'll need to follow through on your words. The true measure of your character will rest with your action, not mere words.

But you'll need to be strong, and develop a close, mutually respectful relationship with your kids before you can expect to demand good moral behaviors from them.

Eleven

Education—The Key to a Really Great Future!

Not too long ago I asked a twelve year old, the daughter of an old acquaintance, what she'd like to be when she grew up!

"Sir," she replied, "I'd like to have lots of things to look forward to and enjoy: set goals that need to be met; own a beautiful home; get married; have children; travel the world and see new places and cultures; give back to my community. I'd also like to understand" she concluded, "how technology really works so I can get involved."

"Do you think she's capable of accomplishing all of these things?" I asked her mom. "Yes, she can," she replied. "But her chosen path will determine whether she does or not."

"She has two options," she said. "Option one: acquire little or no education and begin working in a difficult job—if she can find one—with minimum pay; working longer hours with less time to accomplish anything new; probably live in a rented apartment with time spent there in between jobs; have less time to find a husband, with having children now almost certainly out of the question since they'll need a great deal of time and attention not to mention the cost of raising them."

"Taking vacation time to see the world also seems remote as her low paying job without benefits, and no skill development have now caused her to lose many if not all of the important things she always wanted.

45

"Option two is getting a college education; get a degree and work where she wants to, not where she must; grow into a responsible adult, and do what she feels is right for her own life. She'll have my complete support if she chooses the latter," she concluded.

A good education is an essential starting point for every child—the foundation, if you like, to the kind of future that's every parent's dream! The road traveled isn't easy. But it's filled with amazing possibilities for upward mobility and success. It's no wonder the push for children to excel at school has become so intense.

But where do you begin to create such a world full of possibilities for them? It all begins with literacy, the ability to read and write well.

And When Does Literacy Begin?

Kids learn to read and write in their most formative years. As they learn to read they start learning how to think abstractly, because words convey ideas and relationships between ideas.

Starting at the early stage is critical and must be encouraged through kindergarten and second grade in particular. As they progress academically if they can't read well, every subject they try to learn will frustrate them. If they can't read math, history, or science textbooks; if they stumble over the words, they may soon give up out of frustration and their entire life can easily degenerate into misery, failure, and hopelessness.

Writing is equally significant. It's a creative endeavor, and like reading, their writing experience may also determine their lifelong attitude.

Most children will begin their writing with artwork. This is normal. Drawings enable them to focus. As they draw, they add certain details and leave others out. What they're doing is telling their story through art, a story they'll later relate in words.

In their primary years many will make progress beyond the normal here, but do not expect too much too quickly, they're still in what is known as the pre-operational stage and must be treated with utmost care.

Their Impressionable Years!

Most of those years will be spent in school. From the moment they enter kindergarten until high school graduation and through college, their waking lives will be shaped by events there: in the classroom, on the playground, even in the crowded corridors on their way in.

There, they'll make their own friends, discover new talents, struggle with their own problems and a whole lot more. And hopefully if all goes well, they'll acquire the skills and knowledge necessary to become more than who they were and ensure their own success beyond school.

Your Role in Their Success

How much we work to stimulate them at home goes a long way toward their educational development and there's a lot you can do to help, including certain skill preparation in advance that'll not only ease their transition from home to school, but will also make their school experience far more rewarding.

In so doing, it is important to remember that the goals of the school are both academic and social which includes how to be responsible members of a group: share materials; take turns; be quiet when required to; take care of belongings; cooperate with others in accomplishing tasks.

All of these skills, and more, will be needed as she continues her schooling hence the need to think in terms of social behavior as well as academic readiness.

Helping Them at Home

Let's Begin by Keeping Them Healthy

Getting your kids to eat more fruit and vegetable—as opposed to eating chicken nuggets and French fries—and doing routine exercise are very, very important to their health. Let's talk a little, however, about sleep deprivation, lack of sufficient sleep, which is a rampant problem among teens in particular. Not only is it a major factor in the undermining of children's health, but it has also been shown to cause difficulties in school: disciplinary problems, sleepiness in class, poor concentration and lower grades.

According to Cornell University psychologist James B. Maas, PhD, one of the nation's leading sleep experts, "Nearly all teenagers as they reach puberty, become walking zombies because they get far too little sleep!"

I can't agree more. For most kids, the alarm clock goes off by 6:30 A.M., a scant seven hours after they went to bed. Many board the school bus before 7 A.M. and are in class by 7:30.

In adults, such meager sleep allowances are known to affect day-to-day functioning in myriad ways. In adolescents, who are biologically driven to sleep longer and later than adults do, the effects are likely to be even more dramatic—so much so that some sleep experts contend that the nation's early high school start times, increasingly common, are tantamount to abuse.

And according to the National Highway Traffic Safety Administration, out of the more than 100,000 traffic accidents each year caused by drowsiness and fatigue, young drivers are at the wheel in more than half of these crashes.

While it is true, that many children will, of their own volition, take measures to ensure they get all of the sleep they need, many will not. Here's where you as a parent comes in. Hopefully, you'll do all within your power to ensure that they do.

Helping with School Work

Most schools will do a pretty good job of teaching your kids but their success in school may also depend on how active you work with them at home academically and helping with their homework is one way in which you can.

Once your child is in middle school it is likely that there will be homework nightly. Here are a few suggestions on how you may help:

- Set a fixed time for their homework. Some children need to let off steam after being in school all day, so after dinner may be the right time to start. Others get tired early, so homework may need to begin shortly after school. Work out with her what time is best, come to an agreement and make a routine out of it.
- Help her find the best place to work and make that the Homework Place.
- Make sure there are supplies (pens, pencil, paper, etc.) at her study. It'll help her get settled down quicker when everything is within reach.
- Some children need complete quiet while others may need soft music in the background. Low music is fine, but the television should be off during homework at all times.
- Ask her at least once a month if there's any big project going on at school. If there is, ask her to bring home an outline and post it where it's visible. Put a calendar in her bedroom and have her mark the start date of the project.

49

- As much as possible allow her to have some control over homework time. Offer suggestions, but let her make the decision on how she'll work.

QUESTION: What if she came home and said, "Mom, there's no homework today?"

Create some! Make up some math facts she's been having problems with; have her write out some words and put them in a sentence, or have her do some reading. You'll be surprised how this will in turn, make her decide, that bringing home that work—if there was any—is well worth it!

Keeping Their Confidence Level High Is Also Important and Here Are a Few Things You Can Do

- Raise or lower their performance bar as necessary, depending on their abilities and things that may be impacting their lives at any given time.
- Create a flexible, supportive environment that fosters self-reliance.
- Do not judge them by grades alone. Grades are important but sometimes the quest for good grades can become an obsession. As parents, we can fall into this common trap which can lead to depression and loss of interest when expectations aren't met.
- Value their motivation or willingness to improve.
- Place great value in whatever choices they make for the right reasons.
- Be there for them all times. They'll be happy to have you as a **safety net** when they realize they do not have all of the answers.

Helping Them Prepare for Tests

Whether in grade school, middle school, high school, or for college admissions, testing is an integral part of school life these days. Government funding is, in fact, dependent on the relative overall performance of schools, thus, students are tested periodically along their academic journey.

The foundation of test preparation is learning the material on which students are to be tested, knowing what to expect, and how to get the maximum scores based on the construction of the test and how they are scored.

Some children are at ease when studying for tests while others feel pressured. For the pressured child, studying can then become a chore which in turn can cause her to do poorly in areas where she'd otherwise excel.

How You Can Help?

1. First, explain to your kids that everyone handles studying differently, that everyone has strong points and weak points, and that specific skills such as reading, note taking, handling textbooks, researching and writing reports, organization, even time management, can all have a dramatic impact on their performance.
2. Make a point that cramming doesn't work, that a little bit of studying each night will bring better results than trying to cram an entire chapter or book in one fell swoop.
3. Teachers usually offer a lot of pre-test information. Remind them to listen and follow all guidelines and encourage them to look over their notes before taking a test, if time permits.
4. Help them understand test-taking strategies such as how to approach multiple choices.

5. Encourage them to skip any trouble spots (the questions to which they do not readily have the answers). Failure to do so may result in them having to rush answers to the remaining questions and risk getting poor results. They can always return to that trouble spot if time permits.
6. Teach them to remember the clue words about a given subject. Often, they'll read through a chapter for instance, and become overwhelmed just thinking that they need to remember every word. When it comes to a vocabulary test for instance, they may be given a paper that contains a number of words in one column and the definitions in another. Those definitions are usually the clue words.
7. Make sure they go to bed early the night before a test.
8. Do your best to help them overcome anxiety.

For additional help with test preparation and test preparation resources visit: http://www.kaptest.com/

Working with Teachers

Working in harmony with your child's teacher can benefit her in both social and academic terms and many anecdotal stories and research findings support this view.

"No matter how dedicated and committed are school staff" according to Networker 2000, "they'll get only lackluster results if parents weren't behind the results."

Your child's teacher is someone who should have your confidence and utter respect if the partnership is to work well. It requires regular communication and some of the benefits include:

• Her teacher being informed about cultural background

and other pertinent information that can be useful in working with her
- Her teacher being notified of family problems that may spill over in the classroom
- You being supplied with written reports of infractions if or when they occur
- . . . and a whole lot more . . .

Of equal importance in that team effort is the need to be involved in her school activities where possible and in her school life overall including the attending of PTA conferences and other school meetings.

In 1996 an education department survey found that where parents were highly involved in their child's school, 51 percent of children got mostly A's as opposed to 27 percent where parents' involvement was low.

Financing Their College Education

College is one of the biggest expenses you'll face and the cost varies widely. A four-year private college can cost $25,000 per year or more with a four-year public college in the $10,000 per-year range.

And how do you prepare for such expense? Many parents do it primarily by setting up a specific savings plan. Federal Parents Loans with low interest rates are also available with the advantage of spreading the costs over time.

Financial aid is also available through grants, scholarships and student loans. Grants and scholarships are monies that do not have to be repaid while student loan rates are generally lower than rates for other types of loans. They're repaid after the student finishes college. Some colleges also offer work-study programs where students can work during the summer to help pay their college expenses.

Often, it isn't easy. But the short-term hardship of paying for a college education is obviously outweighed by long-term rewards.

According to a U.S. Census Bureau Report in 2002, on average, workers who graduated high school earned a yearly salary of $26,800. Those with a bachelor's degree earned an average yearly income of $50,650, and those with degrees in business, law, or medicine, earned on a average $101,400.

Of course, your son may decide he wants to be a forklift operator at a local marina, making $19 an hour. $19 an hour may seem like a fortune to a younger teenager yes, but what'll happen when he grows up and gets married, wants to own a beautiful home, have children, and wants to travel the world?

It cannot be stressed enough to young people that a college education is the only way to obtain a good job, the type of job that'll allow for a comfortable lifetime income and a secure future. It's the thin line between living a full life with all of their dreams at their fingertips, and living with a sense of insecurity or merely just getting by.

The path is theirs to choose and hopefully you'll be there to guide them all the way until they realize their dreams, and full potential.

Twelve

The Effects of Peer Pressure and How You Can Help

Making friends and fitting in are an important part of growing up. Among other things they help form the basis for relationships we build with others both present and future.

For your kids it's no different. They want to be accepted, to belong, and to be like peers they admire, which, more often than not, is a good thing. Just by spending time together they learn a lot from each other—even when they disagree, while working out their differences or by simply saying no about being asked to do something wrong.

A lot will depend on what matters or what's important to the kids they spend time with. But at some point, pressures to conform—to their wishes, desires, etc. will arise. This is known as peer pressure.

Peer pressure is more than just a phase that young people go through. It can be a negative force in the lives of children and adolescents, often resulting in behaviors disapproved of by their parents such as skipping school, experimentation with tobacco, alcohol, and illegal drugs.

But peer pressure isn't always negative and many young people benefit from good or positive peer pressure—studying for a test, signing up for a new activity, eating healthy foods, or volunteering for a community service project.

Good or bad, however, it's one thing that all children face. No matter how popular or how well liked they are, it's inescapable.

When Does Peer Pressure Begin?

It begins as early as nursery school when one child simply wants another to play a certain game regardless of whether he/she wishes to play that game or not. By middle and high school, it changes somewhat, progressing, if you like, into conforming to group norms (such as wearing certain types of clothes, or simply alienating another teen). And depending on what a group of kids thinks is cool, yours may be swayed to break rules or try something risky at times, even if it's just for the fun of doing it.

Responding to Peer Pressure

Not all teenagers respond to peer group pressure in the same way: 11 to 14-year-olds appear to be more influenced by it than older teenagers.

There are also important individual differences to take into account. Some teenagers, for instance, are simply more independent-minded than others and are better at withstanding such pressures. Research indicates that the ones who are most affected by it are those who receive little or no support at home.

Why Do Kids Give in to Peer Pressure?

1. To be liked; to fit in.
2. Worry about being made fun of if they don't conform.
3. Curiosity: want to try something new.

4. Unsure about what they believe and where they stand about their own place in the world.
5. A need for new values and attitudes. They look to their peers to provide alternatives.
6. Group influence: Many spend a lot of time in groups—either in school, sport or other leisure activities.
7. Experiment: In the process of becoming adults, teenagers want to experiment somewhat—with drug and alcohol use, sexual behavior and so on, something entirely new to which they tend to look to their peers for guidance.
8. Low self-esteem; lack of confidence; feeling isolated from peers and/or family.
9. Poor academic abilities or performance and lack of direction in life.

But All Isn't Lost

Given the right support, kids can become resilient. They can learn to say no and there are numerous ways in which you, as a parent, can help.

Providing Support

Two major sources of support—family and friends, are critical. Often, just being able to talk through things will help a teenager understand how he's being pressured unfairly or unnecessarily. It is important here, that you keep all channels of communication open.

A good friend (a friend of the kid) may also be useful in helping your teen get things into perspective. Together they may also be able to stand up against the peer group in question—much easier than one.

Boost his/her social development. Teach her how to form positive relationships. Research shows that the pressure to use tobacco, alcohol, and illegal drugs comes most often from wanting to be accepted, wanting to belong, and wanting to be noticed. Show her what qualities to look for in a friend, and advise her about what to say if offered harmful substances. If she has difficulty making friends she'll need your support even more.

Teaching Them Refusal Skills Is a Great Defense

Start by asking: "What do you do when someone tries to get you to do something you do not want to do? If offered, would you drink beer at your best friend's birthday party? Or would you be comfortable at a graduation party where wine is being offered to underage kids?"

Do a number of role-play situations in which you pose as the one making the offer and have them practice different ways to say "no."

Continue the exercise until they feel confident that they have the power to make the right choice.

NOTE: Different aged children may face different situations, and it is important to make sure they practice with situations that may actually arise.

Ways to Say No

Teach them how to refuse offers of cigarettes, alcohol and drugs. Help them feel comfortable with saying "NO." A shy kid may feel more at ease saying, "no thanks," or "I have to go," while the more outgoing kid may say something more candid such as, "forget it!" or "no way!"

Talk to them about how to avoid undesirable situations or people bent on breaking rules.

Let them know that it is okay to seek adult advice. While it would be ideal that they sought yours, other trusted adults can also be of help.

You, the Kids, Party and Alcohol

During the busy prom and graduation season, your teens may be invited to a party where alcohol will be available to minors. But kids, parties, and alcohol are never a good mix and here are a few steps you can take to keep your child alcohol free:

1. Before the party, talk with the parents hosting the party and get all the details. Where is it? What time does it begin and end? Who's invited? What activities are planned? Will there be adult supervision for teenage guests? What is the ratio of adult supervisors to teenage guests? What can I do to help? Do NOT see yourself as being nosy! Think of it as information gathering or fact finding in an effort to make an informed decision.

2. Ask if alcohol will be served at the event. If it's a party with guests over and under age twenty-one and alcohol will be present, ask about their plans to prevent minors from drinking. If all of the guests will be under twenty-one, ask about their plans to make sure that no one sneaks in alcohol or be allowed to use any.

3. Talk to your child about what to do if alcohol is available to minors. Let her know that even if other teens are drinking, you expect her not to. Tell her that she should call you right away and you'll come pick her up—no matter how late it is. Create a "code word" that she can use as she may be calling you when surrounded by friends during that call.

Yes, at times you may have to make difficult choices about

what parties your kids attend. It can be hard to tell them "no" at times when "everyone" else is going along. You may even wonder if you've set the bar too high.

But it's okay to be tough when it comes to protecting your kids. Underage drinking is a key factor in the two leading causes of teenage deaths: car accidents and fatal injuries. It's also linked to two-thirds of all sexual assaults and date rapes in teens, and increases the chances of contracting HIV or sexually transmitted diseases.

Final Note

Children and adolescents outside of situations where they feel pressured into negative acts are far less likely to commit such acts. Likewise, those who choose friends who do not smoke, drink, use drugs, steal, and lie to their parents are far less likely to do these things.

Remind your child therefore, that there is strength in numbers. When young people can anticipate stressful peer pressure situations, it might be helpful if they rounded up as many friends as they can, play the numbers game if you like. There's truly strength in numbers.

Part IV

When the Going Gets Tough

- Sibling Rivalry
- Handling Misbehavior
- How Well Do You Know Your Child?
- Spanking—Does It Really Work?

Thirteen
Sibling Rivalry

"Get out of my chair!"

"Dad, Susan won't give my teddy back!"

"Mom, he's in my room digging into my things again!"

And on and on it goes . . .

Sound familiar? If you have more than one child, it probably does. It's the sound of sibling rivalry. While many siblings are lucky enough to become the best of friends, it's very common for brothers and sisters to fight.

What Is Sibling Rivalry?

Sibling rivalry—one of the inevitable annoyances of having children—is the jealousy, competition, personality clashes, antagonism, hostility or fighting between brothers and/or sisters. Whether it's about needing space, asserting independence or whatever the reason, one minute there could be a deafening silence at home, the next minute the house could be turned into a war zone.

And although it is common for them to swing back and forth

between adoring and detesting each other, at times they can literally drive you crazy to the point where you feel like disappearing forever.

Sibling rivalry is one of humanity's oldest problems. It began with two brothers, Abel and Cain, as told in one of the first stories in the Bible. See Genesis 4:1–6.

As the story goes, the older brother, Cain, was irritated at constantly having to help take care of his younger brother, Abel. So angry, that at some point he even asked his parents: "Am I my brother's keeper?" Finally, he became so angry that he killed his only brother, Abel.

That was of course, an extreme case of sibling rivalry. But the fact that it is one of the first stories written in the Bible goes to show the great importance given to the subject itself.

Why Do They Fight?

There are lots of reasons why siblings fight. Often it's about some degree of jealousy or competition. But there are other factors—factors which may even influence how often and how severe the fighting gets. They include:

- **Individual temperaments.** Individual temperaments including mood, disposition, and adaptability—and their unique personalities—play a large role in how well siblings get along. One child may be laid back while another is easily rattled. That alone is more than enough to set them off. Similarly, a child who is particularly clingy and drawn to parents (to mom in particular), for comfort and love might be resented by other siblings who'd want the same kind or the same amount of attention.
- **Age difference.** A three year old for instance simply won't have the language or capacity for logical reasoning.

Try explaining the need for her to love and care for her new brother or sister and the only thing she'll understand is her own frustration and anger with the arrival of this new "intruder" into the family, all of a sudden.

- **Evolving needs.** It's natural for kids' changing needs, anxieties, and identities to affect how they relate to one another. Toddlers for instance, are naturally protective of their toys and belongings. This is the stage at which they're learning to assert their will, and they'll do it at every turn.
- **Favoritism.** Favoritism is also one of the main causes of conflict among kids! Unfortunately, we tend to play "choice games" at times. But kids will pick up on this disparity and react. Having a close bond with a particular child or enjoying each of your children in different ways is not favoritism, but treating them in terms of a hierarchy, emotionally, is!

So is there anything you can do to maintain harmony and peace at home?

Of course every home is different and the misbehaviors and consequences may undoubtedly be different. But like every parent I'm sure you hate the atmosphere of tension that invariably follows these often bitter exchanges.

Fortunately, you can take steps that'll help your kids get along with lasting peace that'll benefit everyone.

Let's begin with some basics including things to avoid:

- Never compare your kids.
- Do not typecast. Let them be themselves.
- Never ever play favorites. We've discussed this already but it is really important. It is one of the main causes of conflict among kids!
- Set them up to cooperate rather than compete.

- Pay attention to the time of day and other patterns in *which* conflicts usually occur. Perhaps a change of routine, an earlier meal or snack, or a well-planned activity when the kids are at loose ends could help.
- Teach them positive ways to get attention from each other.
- Be fair: This is very important. Your children need to know that you'll do your best to meet each of their unique needs.
- Plan family activities that are fun for everyone. It's easier to work with someone with whom warm memories are shared.

Be there for each child: Set aside "alone time" for each child. Try to get in at least a few minutes each day. It's amazing how much even just ten minutes of uninterrupted one-on-one time can mean to a child.

Involve them in setting ground rules for acceptable behavior: ground rules, with clear and consistent consequences for breaking them can help prevent many squabbles. Here are some suggestions:

1. No hurting (hitting, kicking, punching, etc.) is allowed
2. No name-calling, yelling, or tattling is allowed
3. If they fight over a toy, the toy goes into time-out
4. Whoever demands to be first, will go last
5. No making fun of anyone who is punished

Have fun together as a family: Not only is this a peaceful way for your kids to spend time together and relate to each other it can help ease tensions between them and also keep you involved.

Resolving conflicts:

- **Do not always intervene:** Research shows that while you should pay attention to your kids' conflicts (so that no one gets hurt), it's best not to intervene. When parents jump in they tend to protect one child (usually the younger sibling) against the other. This often creates resentment by the older and leads to an escalation of the conflict.

- Help them develop skills that'll enable them to work out conflicts on their own. Teach them how to compromise, respect each other, divide things fairly, etc., and express your confidence that they can work it out. Don't get drawn in.
- Don't yell or lecture. It won't help.
- Hold each child equally responsible when ground rules get broken regardless of who started it. It takes two to make a quarrel.
- Give them a chance to express their feelings about each other, but without yelling, name-calling, or violence.
- Encourage win-win negotiations, where each side gains something.
- Recognize when they need time apart from each other and away from family dynamics. Try arranging separate play dates or activities for each kid occasionally. This will also give you an opportunity to spend one-on-one time with the other.

When should you intervene?

- Well, dangerous fights need to be stopped immediately. Make it clear that no violence is ever allowed.
- If they're physically violent with each other, and/or one child's always the victim and doesn't fight back. That is sibling abuse. You may need to seek professional help here.

And finally, promote sibling harmony through family meetings. A family meeting is the coming together for the purpose of allowing all family members to help make family decisions and choices by working together as a team. Parents, children, and any others who live in the home and have a stake in decisions affecting the daily life of the family should participate. Choose a time that is agreeable to everyone.

The meetings may comprise of two leadership roles: (1) a chairperson who keeps the discussion on track and sees that everyone's opinion is heard and (2) a secretary who'll take notes, write them up and read them in the form of minutes at the next meeting. Parents can assume these duties at the first meeting or at the early stage allowing other family members to take turns so that no one has total responsibility for every task.

Family meetings help to build cooperation and responsibility, while making anger and rebellion less likely. It's also a time to share love, develop unity, and build trust.

Fourteen
Handling Misbehavior

As parents we all hope we'll end up with the ideal child, one that does his homework all of the time, never misbehaves, and above all, live in a home with no screaming, no fighting, no tension whatsoever. No doubt this may have been your dream for years. But you must parent the child you have not the one you wish you had.

For a variety of reasons, many still unknown, all children display undesirable forms of misbehavior at some point, or from time to time. How best to manage such behavior is often complex and what will work for one child won't necessarily work for another.

No formal parenting skills training in and of itself could fully prepare you for the baffling events surrounding child development, and its many challenges may test you to the limit! Fortunately there are steps you can take to guide them along a positive path, even at a time when they're being pulled in so many different directions.

First of all when children misbehave, it's generally a cry for help. Their behavior is telling us about a need, a need for some autonomy perhaps. OR, a need to feel safe; feel accepted; feel loved or appreciated; they may also be experiencing a variety of feelings for the first time, and become deeply troubled about what may have gone wrong.

As a parent it is our responsibility to:

1. Recognize the misbehavior, and the need.

2. Respond appropriately instead of trying to simply maintain power by yelling for instance, or handing out punishments that may have little impact on teens in particular, especially if they believe that the situation doesn't warrant such reactions.

In recognizing and dealing with their misbehavior it is also important to recognize that children's needs, wants, desires, abilities, and indeed, their own view of the world may be quite different from yours.

You must also become aware of the various phases that all children go through as they grow and develop and learn about the world around them; and that each phase may bring with it its own difficulties for both child and parent.

It is important that you as a parent understand these things. And the reason this is so important, is that unless you take into account all of these variables, among others, it is unlikely that you'll decide on the best possible age-appropriate way to respond.

1. Start by Looking and Listening for Needs

You need to understand why your child acts the way he or she does. That must be done first or it'll become difficult, if not impossible to teach appropriate behavior that'll lead to change. Certain basic understandings will be helpful here.

Depending on his temperament for instance, tackling misbehavior head-on might be counterproductive. He may already be consumed with rage and anger and such approach in itself can become a source of tension—or worse. Taking an approach that encourages characteristics such as awareness and problem solving, may on the other hand, lead to results that'll even astound you.

An approach in the form of a game can help. A good example of this might be **The Nose Watching Game.**

In case you haven't heard of "Nose Watching" before, "Nose Watching" is designed to train children to be aware of other people's noses. While out in public, have them look at how many different kinds of noses they can observe so that later you can both discuss the different nose types they may have seen and hopefully agree that no two were alike. We'll talk some more about "Nose Watching" in a moment and how to use it as a behavior modification tool. But first . . .

HERE ARE A FEW OF THE COUNTLESS REASONS WHY A CHILD MAY BE ACTING THE WAY HE/SHE DOES:

- Has too much stimulation
- Feels bored
- Feels frustrated
- Needs attention
- Has little impulse control
- Lacks the ability to put feelings into words
- Thinks it's the best way to get what he/she wants
- Doesn't clearly understand the rules
- Testing you, or to gain your attention
- Can't have his/her way
- Needs to feel a sense of power and control
- Lack of knowledge or experience about something he/she is forced to do

Their behavior is also influenced strongly by family styles, aspects of culture and the people and environment around them.

2. Don't Overreact

Try to focus on the behavior in a way that does NOT belittle, criticize or shame the child. Although at times we may genuinely feel that we're giving a clear "Stop" message to a child, often, what we do is give a yellow or even green light to more unwanted behaviors. A strong-willed child in particular will find ways to upset or anger you further, especially if he/she enjoys seeing you jump and yell.

Let's return to the "Nose Watching" game. The whole idea behind the game was to create awareness, awareness that no two people are alike; that we are unique with unique characteristics, problems and behaviors with each problem or behavior having its own solution.

Once this is established, break slowly to him the real reason for having him play "Nose Watching" and how it relates to his misbehavior. Ask if he is aware of the behavior in question; if so what does he believe may be the cause, and how you might work together to improve or change it.

Tell him it's an extension of the nose-watching game. Only this time you'll both be looking not at people's noses but at his needs. Explain that needs are a lot like noses but are harder to see. To see needs, he'd have to look hard and listen hard. Someone might be feeling a little discouraged and needs some encouragement; another, a little insecure and needs a compliment. Still, another might be feeling left out and needs a friend, or useless and needs to be asked for help. OR, there might be more obvious needs such as hunger or loneliness.

Tell him also, that when one member of the family is hurt in any way, that every member suffers. And that you both need to find a way to correct what has gone wrong so that it doesn't continue to hurt everyone.

NOTE: Nose-watching also gives a sense of teamwork, as opposed to the feeling of being on opposite sides.

3. Create an Environment That'll Encourage Dialogue

A big part of childhood has to do with learning how to turn

wrongs around and make them right and one way you can help in this regard is by encouraging your kids to talk to you as opposed to fearing you!

- **Start by building a close, trusting relationship.** Often, a good way to begin is by saying something that reaffirms your confidence in their abilities; that you are proud of what they have accomplished, or in their willingness to learn, or change—an affirmation that's good for their self-image and one that'll encourage mature behavior and independence, among other things.
- **Evaluate your communication style**
- **Find occasions where you can talk alone**—one on one away from brother, sister or anyone else. And make sure you listen carefully to what is being said as well as what is not
- **Help express their feelings, including anger**

A huge problem that often surfaces during adolescence in particular, though, is the power struggle that develops between teens and adults, with the kids wanting to feel powerful in an adult world. Often, there's little more than bravado here, a cover-up for their own insecurity. Their know-it-all attitude may be one way of crying out for your guidance.

Recognize it for what it is and find ways to work through it—together.

The big secret? Communicate! Communicate! Communicate! Make a point to talk with them not only when there is a problem but also when there isn't any. Such conversations can be refreshing and insightful. Make them part of your daily routine.

Besides, even children with the worst types of behavior have their good moments. When they are behaving well, they deserve your attention and appreciation too.

73

Preventative Steps That Will Put You Back in the Driver's Seat!

Handling misbehavior is NOT about harsh punishment. It's about giving children clear, respectful messages designed to help make acceptable choices.

Here are a few tips:

1. Set clear guidelines
2. Set limits—respectful limit setting along with clear directions on how to achieve them
3. Build close, trusting relationships not just with the affected child but a better relationship in the home overall
4. Offer reward for good behavior or accomplishments—you decide which rewards are suitable. They may be coupons for special privileges, achievement certificates or even a savings account

NOTE: Bribery is not a healthy or effective form of motivation and there may be a thin line here.

Fifteen

How Well Do You Know Your Child?

As a parent how well do you know your kids? Do you know them well enough to understand their innermost feelings, some of the things they're capable of doing whether you're present or not?

When was the last time you sat down and tried to find out their innermost thoughts? Are you an overinvolved mom or dad who spends way too much time away from home? If you do, there are so many important or illuminating things you probably won't know about them.

Based on an extensive series of interviews with children and parents, Dr. Ron Taffel, psychotherapist, child-rearing expert and author, concludes that too many of today's children remain unseen by parents, and writes: "Stretched to the limits as we are, we do not really know the children we have. We cannot always tell the ways in which they are uniquely different because we just do not spend enough direct, one-to-one time with them."

"Sometimes I get the feeling my parents don't know me," said a fifth grader, interviewed by Dr. Taffel. "Mine, too!" yelled another! "We don't spend time together—we're always so busy in my house!"

Children are often angry and yearn for what they do not get from their parents according to Dr. Taffel. "In my conversation with children from pre-kindergarten to sixth grade" he writes, "the kids overwhelmingly indicated that what they wanted most from their parents was more time, as in undivided attention . . ."

"These are among the many heartfelt responses of children who are desperate to be seen, truly known, rather than scheduled," he concludes.

Discovering Themselves

Children, especially during puberty, begin to discover and develop their own identity. They go through emotional and psychological identity crisis, question and may even silently challenge much of what you say, or what you stand for. This is the point in their lives when they probably need your support and direction most, although it is unlikely they'll ask for it.

And how can you know? You need to find out, and here's an approach you can take: Begin by asking a few searching questions, conversational-style, open-ended questions that won't result in the usual one-word responses. Also, ask specific rather than general questions that'll encourage them to think.

Here's a list of prepared questions that you may use as a guide. Modified from the *Miami Herald*, January 1982, they still work extremely well today. Answer them yourself and then ask your kids—a few at a time if they're very young—and compare the results.

1. Who is your son's best friend?
2. Who is his greatest hero?
3. What would you like your daughter to be when she grows up?
4. Who's her favorite teacher?
5. What's their favorite or least favorite school subject?
6. Do they feel liked by children at school?
7. What's your son's nickname at school?
8. Do your kids prefer to do homework after school, after supper, or in the morning before school?

9. What sports do they enjoy most?
10. What's their favorite TV program?
11. Who outside the immediate family has been most influential in their lives?
12. What chores do they like least?
13. What's their biggest fear?
14. What really makes them angry or sad?
15. What gifts from you do they cherish most?
16. What activities have they enjoyed most in the last month or two?
17. What's their favorite family occasion?
18. Would your kids' first choice for a vacation be a camping trip, a visit to a big city or a boat trip?
19. What foods do they like or dislike most?
20. Which would they prefer as a pet: a cat, a dog, a bird or a fish?
21. What's their favorite music?
22. What's their biggest complaint about the family?
23. What would they most like to change about the family?
24. What about you would they most like to change?
25. Do they feel fairly treated at home?

Even if you're close with your children—regardless of how close you are—there'll always be a number of things you do not know about them . . . unless you ask! This could also be a way for them to get to know you better. Encourage them to ask questions in the process, and have fun!

Things You Should Know That May Be Affecting Your Kids

1. DEPRESSION:
Although depression is less common in children than in

adults, about one in five young people will experience depression before becoming adults and those who do usually have a hard time dealing with everyday activities and responsibilities. This may occur at any point in a child's life, even when things seem to be going well.

2. **EPHEDRA:** Dangerous and Ineffective.

The pressures of competitive high school sports and a culture that values being thin might tempt your teen to try a dietary or sports supplement. Most teens aren't aware of the danger of using supplements but they can be harmful to their health and may even result in death.

3. **POPPING PILLS:**

This is a common problem among kids. They'd find ways to get them legally at local or legitimate online pharmacies but when popping pills becomes a top priority, they will often find new ways to obtain them.

Next, do you know what your kids are up to while spending time with their friends?

Unsupervised children in particular, simply have more opportunities to experiment with risky behaviors, including the use of alcohol, tobacco and illegal drugs, and they may start substance abuse at earlier ages.

Here are a number of tips to help you monitor their activities—without appearing to be a spy:

Hug him as soon as he arrives at home. Check for odors of possible marijuana smoke or alcohol although cologne, aftershave or chewing gum may be used to neutralize the odor.

Teenagers under the influence will usually go straight to their room as they arrive home. While making eye contact, hold a brief conversation. Check for bloodshot eyes, slurred speech and good balance.

Ask what time it is and take a good look at the way he looks at his watch.

If he unexpectedly wants to spend the night at a friend's house, and you have concerns, say no.

Maintain an unpredictable schedule making it difficult for him to plan around your schedule.

Keep abreast of what he does when away from home. Meet with his friends and friends' parents and participate in mutual activities. This form of networking brings surprisingly good results.

Ask your neighbors (the ones you can trust) to discreetly keep an eye on any activities that may take place while you are not home.

Check to see how he's doing at school. Ask his teacher if there is any cause for concern.

Ask his friends to identify themselves when they call. Encourage him to invite them over while you're at home. Get to know them.

Monitor His Activities Online

Unfortunately the same advances in computer and telecommunication technology that allow our children to reach out to new sources of knowledge and cultural experiences are also leaving them vulnerable to exploitation and harm.

They're the first generation to grow up digital, and expressing themselves through the computer and the Internet has become the norm. But with every stranger in the world potentially having access to your child, right in your own home, what can you do? A lot!

One way to begin is to purchase an Activity Monitoring Software such as Web Watcher that'll allow you to see what he's doing in real time. Web Watcher comes with features that'll allow you to:

- Block Web pages or access to Web content

- Read Instant Message (IM or "Chat") Conversations
- Read Incoming and Outgoing E-mail
- Log every keystroke
- Record online & offline activities and more

And with Web Watcher you can monitor all of their online activities from any Internet connected PC from anywhere in the world. Get details at http://www.awarenesstech.com/

Sixteen

Spanking—Does It Really Work?

Around six and a half months ago, I raised this question during a frank discussion with a group of parents many of whom I've had the pleasure of working with for sometime.

Not surprisingly, there were as many shades of opinions on the subject as were the number of parents involved with many offering their own rationale for what opponents of spanking or corporal punishment often refer to as parental brutality.

Many argued for instance, that "it's the only thing we can do at times," while others recounted that "as children we've all been spanked."

But in spite of their own spanking experiences—and repressed feelings of humiliation, resentment and crippling feelings of helplessness and despair—around 80 percent of the group still believed, almost to a fault, that spanking was an acceptable form of punishment on moral or religious grounds sanctioned by the book of Proverbs: "He that spares the rod hates his son . . . " (Proverbs 13:24).

Since 1995, spanking has become a high-profile controversy in North America.

Proponents of corporal punishment of children and over-the-top disciplinarians for instance—whilst accepting that excessive physical punishment amounts to child abuse—argue that spanking, properly administered, is an effective form of discipline for unruly children and a way to reassert control over young adolescents in particular. They further argue that abandoning child discipline in the form of spanking will lead to lawlessness and violence in society when a child reaches adulthood.

Spanking appears so ingrained in our society, in fact, that numerous polls confirm that the overwhelming majority of Americans believe it is sometimes necessary, and that around 90 percent of parents continue to use it as a form of punishment. But does spanking really work? There's overwhelming evidence to the contrary.

Consistent with previous studies opponents of spanking have found it to be dangerous and ineffective. Researcher and sociologist Murray Straus in a recent study for instance, found "corporal punishment" to be counter-productive, resulting in misbehavior, resentment and mistrust and in the *Medical Journal Archives of Pediatrics and Adolescent Medicine,* Straus wrote: "We want to know, when parents spank does behavior change for the worse, for the better or is there no difference? What we found," concludes Straus, "was that it changes behavior for the worse."

The use of the word *spanking* as a definition for the discipline of children appears to be largely a North American term. In Britain for instance, it is generally referred to as *smacking*.

Call it what you will, whilst the practice is accepted—and embraced—in many countries, it is also illegal in many others with mounting pressures in countries such as the UK, to have it—in whatever form—made illegal and treated as child abuse while countries such as Sweden, Finland, Norway, Austria, Cyprus, Denmark, Latvia and others, have outlawed the practice altogether.

Here in the United States, making it an illegal act is still fiercely resisted, from conservatives in particular, although most child psychologists, religious liberals and others now oppose the measure in favor of other disciplinary methods.

I can't agree more. In my own practice, I've found that a large number of adults who now suffer from acute depression have suffered some form of corporal punishment at some point during their childhood.

While the overall causes of their condition remained inconclusive for the most part, objective research definitely shows, that even moderate spanking can have devastating effects including anxiety, depression and drug and alcohol addiction for many children—particularly males—during adulthood. This is no longer a matter of opinion and the stakes are high!

When you spank, what you do is introduce chaos into your child's world. It says to that child that violence is an appropriate manner in which to react when you're mad. If they then conclude that spanking is an acceptable form of punishment, it is reasonable to believe that when they themselves become adults, they will be more likely to perpetuate that cycle of violence with their own children.

I've said this earlier but it is so important. I'll say it again. Child discipline is not about harsh punishment and often we need to take a look at ourselves as our children are to a large extent, a mirror of what we are.

As a former teacher myself—and parent—I often found myself yelling and searching for stricter forms of punishments to get children to cooperate or to perform better. They never worked and I soon realized that I needed to find a new approach, a change of behavior, my behavior. If I were to expect change in the behavior of others I'd have to change my behavior first.

I did—through relationship-building measures as opposed to force. I can therefore say with certainty that it worked nearly every time and may address many of the questions of why some youngsters make a successful transition into adulthood while others do not.

Part V

Parenting for Tomorrow

- Single Parenting
- Fathers Have a Role to Play Too
- Grandparenting and the Benefits to a Child

Seventeen
Single Parenting

One half of our society will experience single parenting in one form or another and if you're a single parent my heart goes out to you. Whether through separation, divorce, widowhood, adoption or perhaps just being the "never-married mom/dad," life in your world can be a harrowing experience at times! I never lose sight of how much of a challenge it can be.

One of the problems I find with this family structure is that it continues to be viewed as an oddity, as being inferior, even defective in spite of its prevalence.

It is important, however, that you do not feel or perceive yourself as lesser or defective because of your singleness.

I frequently work with single parents myself and have great admiration and respect for each of them, the women in particular. I think they do not get enough credit for their ability to juggle between being homemaker, employee, nurturer, provider, guardian, protector, etc. while dealing with personal anger or depression and the child's feelings about what is more often than not, a great loss; for their ability to cope with their own ups and downs, past hurts, current fears, uncertain future and more.

Single parenting isn't exclusive to mothers by the way, and the number of single parent fathers is on the rise too, which may surprise you as much as how well they are adjusting to their "new" role.

Not only do they take responsibility for house cleaning and

other mundane tasks, they also report spending lots of time with their children in both household chores and recreational activities.

But there are a variety of problems in single parenting.

The main ones according to Richards & Schmiege (1993) are: money, task overload, social life, and ex-spouse difficulties. For single mothers, money was the biggest problem, up to seventy-eight percent compared to eighteen percent for single fathers. Not much has changed since.

Often single parents also find that they are isolated in a coupled world. And because most households become that way after a divorce or death, there can be painful transitions with effects on the mood, morale, and behavior of both parent and child.

The children themselves often go through a rainbow of emotions: worry, anger, jealousy, fear, withdrawal and feelings of rejection.

Elective single parenting does not have to deal with divorce or death but the child still experiences a loss—emotional as well as physical loss.

Life itself doesn't always turn out the way we planned it and at times when the reality of having to do it alone sinks in, you may feel as if the world is caving in on you. But life must go on regardless and here's a list of suggestions that may be a source of support. Many of these have worked well for other single parent families, after separation or loss, in particular. Hopefully they'll work for you.

1. **Develop a support network.**

Start by acknowledging that you can't do it all and that you can't do it alone. This is absolutely critical. Your network may include immediate family members and friends but think about other people in your life who may also be willing to lend their support. Can someone take the kids out to dinner occasionally, for instance? You need to know who you can depend on.

2. **Be there for your kids.**

Enjoy your children. Get into the habit of talking with them every day. Cherish every moment spent together. Make a special effort to be emotionally present with them. It would be easy to retreat into your heart right now, but your children will need you more than ever. Simple activities such as playing an indoor game or two, or taking a walk together can go a long way toward reassuring them that life will go on and that they will, indeed, be okay.

3. Grieve.

Whether you've experienced the loss of a spouse, the end of a marriage, or an adjustment to the dream you once held for your life, you may experience grief, anger, guilt, loneliness and despair. It is important to grieve and process the loss before attempting to move on.

4. Pay attention to your physical health.

At times you may feel particularly drained. Try eating healthy foods and find ways to keep your body energized. Try taking a walk at lunchtime. Getting adequate rest is also important. It is important to your health overall.

5. Identify what gives you strength.

How have you handled challenging situations in the past? What most energizes you and reminds you that you possess the strength needed to meet your current challenges? Focus on what has worked and find some more. Likewise, let go of what hasn't worked.

6. Focus on the positive.

Take some time to think about the things that are going well for you. Having a positive attitude—even in the midst of extreme circumstances—can empower you to move on and provide your children with a tangible example of the coping strategies you may also want them to adopt.

7. Schedule time to be alone.

It is important that you create pockets of time for yourself when you can *just be*; time when you're not accountable for accomplishing tasks; time to sit; time to think; time to ponder.

8. **Remember to ask for help.**

It is important to know when to ask for help and who you can rely on when you do ask. But never be afraid to ask. Often this may seem like the most difficult thing to do. I know. But simply drawing up a list of the many people who'll be there for you will help remind you that you're not alone. Giving others a chance to help you is both a gift to yourself and to those assisting you. Sharing in each other's lives during difficult times affirms our human connection and brings a sense of purpose to everyday living.

In addition, consider joining a formal single parent support group. They come in all shapes and sizes and many offer a variety of excellent programs for single moms and dads. Before you decide which one(s) to join, however, you'll want to consider your unique needs and compare them to the distinct features of each.

9. **Seek counseling if you need it.**

If you have difficulty functioning or relating to your children, you definitely need to see someone about it. If you feel sad all of the time or can't "see a way out," that's another reason. Get help!

FINAL NOTE: Single parenting especially in the case of separation or divorce affects the entire family, the parent with custody rights, the one with visitation rights, and the children themselves.

It is important therefore—if possible—that everyone maintains a healthy relationship not only for the children's sake, but yours.

I know how difficult it can get when life has knocked you down, perhaps many times. When you think of how much worse it could have been, though, be thankful for what it is!

Eighteen
Fathers Have a Critical Role to Play Too

The magic of motherhood can never, ever be forgotten. While mothers are to be applauded for their unconditional devotion, and whatever sacrifices they make for their children every day, fathers also have a unique and special place in their children's lives. Just being "there" when they need you is, in fact one of the most precious gifts you can give.

You have a unique responsibility to help shape their young lives especially during their formative years or at a time when they're beginning to discover themselves!

Even if you're an absentee father—not currently sharing the same home with that child—abdicating your role or responsibility isn't an option. How much she longs for that moment, that last second when you walk back into her life bringing back the smiles, hope, certainty and the security that only a father can provide!

Toys and gifts may soon wear out, and they do, but whatever you do (or not do) at these critical stages will almost certainly impact that young, even lonely life—not just in the present but into adulthood, even way into the so-called golden years!

Preparing for Fatherhood

So many factors will influence your parental task that perhaps nothing could fully prepare you for such a role.

91

As a father myself I do recall being totally unprepared for the many challenges of helping to raise my own children.

At times in fact, I felt it a near impossibility accomplishing what I naively thought was going to be easy—although in retrospect, it seems easy compared to the challenges and complexities of being a father in this current complex society. But there's hope!

Pre-birth Considerations

One of the secrets to good parenting is to look into the many emotional issues that will arise with the birth of a child, of suddenly having a new baby at home; the importance of anticipating possible changes in the relationship between your partner and you that often seem to catch so many men by surprise.

Such preparation is critical. But as men, we tend to shy away when it comes to issues of the heart, and the result can be that we often feel isolated upon becoming that new parent.

Fathering itself is a daily task and our responsibilities are many and varied ranging from being up at nights helping with the needs of your newborn to having to earn a living to provide for food, shelter and more; from coping with hard discipline situations that arise from time to time to the emotional "battles" faced with several children clamoring for your attention all at once.

It begins with establishing a sound father-child relationship—from the outset. Honesty must be the main thrust of that relationship and getting that message across is critical. One way to do so is by telling a little story about honesty itself, or the flip side and its consequences.

It works, nearly always, and in their book *Teaching Your Children Values,* Linda and Richard Eyre provide a good example of how one lie for instance, can lead to another and produce serious consequences. They've done it using a short story called "Isabel's Little Lie."

It's a story about a child who wasn't supposed to have fed her dinner to her dog, but she did. And when her mother came in and saw her plate all clean, Isabel said that she had eaten it all. (That was a little lie!) The dinner was chicken, and Barker (her dog) ended up with a bone stuck in his throat. Pretty soon he began coughing, snorting and acting very uncomfortably.

"Do you know what's wrong with Barker?" asked her mother. "No," said Isabel, which was another lie but Isabel had to, so that Mother wouldn't find out she'd told the first lie.

Mother looked into Barker's mouth but couldn't see anything. "Did Barker eat something?" asked her mother again. "I don't know Mommy." (Another lie but she didn't want her mother to know about the first two lies.)

Barker's condition got worse, and Mother took him to the animal hospital. Isabel went too. "What happened to the dog?" asked the animal doctor. "We don't know," said Isabel. (That was yet another lie, but if Isabel had told the truth then, Mother and the dog doctor would know she had lied before.)

Then said the doctor, "If it's just a bone, we could get it out with an instrument but it might be glass, so we may have to operate."

Finally, Isabel decided it was time to tell the truth. She exclaimed, "It's a bone! I *did* know Barker had eaten it, and I didn't eat all of my dinner . . . I did give it to Barker, and I won't tell lies anymore because if you tell one, you may have to tell another . . . and another." She then began to cry, but importantly, she decided there and then, that she really would tell the truth from then on.

Unfortunately, fatherhood doesn't come with an instruction manual and ready or not there's a lot to do.

The day your child starts pre-school how will you cope—or help your spouse cope—with the pangs of adult separation anxiety for instance? At what age should you introduce him/her to computers? How do you learn to share control without compromising authority and how do you decide what issues are negotiable, nonnegotiable, and how do you choose your battles with the greatest care?

When a child finishes high school or college and lands a job, your responsibility doesn't necessarily end there either. He/she won't necessarily become that autonomous, responsible adult suddenly. Although they might appear to function as adults in many respects—and they may even act more grown up than they truly are so that you won't have to worry about them—in reality they're often in turmoil, depressed, overwhelmed by life itself; trapped in their childhood years for one reason or another and unable to cope on their own.

There's when they'd really need your support. What will you do? How will you cope?

These questions and hundreds more will arise and the answers won't always be easy. You won't get everything right all of the time. But one way to learn is by listening, observing, and learning from each mistake. You'll also become a role model, so be strong.

Nineteen

Grandparenting and the Benefits to a Child

Instead of a quiet retirement, sweetened by delights of occasional visits, baby-sitting perhaps OR, even spoiling their grandchildren a little, each year, more and more grandparents from all areas, socio-economic or ethnic groups are becoming primary or secondary caregivers. Across the United States, in fact, around one in twelve children now live in households headed by grandparents or other relatives, just like you.

Many have stepped into this vital role even at a moment's notice, often putting many of their plans, even their own retirement, on hold. So, if you were called upon to fill this often enviable—or unenviable—role at a critical time perhaps, you're not alone.

And it doesn't matter whether biological, step or through adoption. It'll make little difference to a child; children understand love, not labels.

Historically, grandparents have provided a safe, stable and nurturing environment for their grandchildren, just as they did when they were parents the first time around. There's hardly a greater opportunity in fact, to watch your grandchildren develop through all stages of growth.

For decades, such kinship care has remained for the most part, informal and unrecognized by the welfare system for instance, as a vital resource for children although, according to the New York City Department for the Aging, grandparents now head nearly 63 percent of the city's kinship foster homes, an unprecedented growth which has its roots in the child welfare act of 1980.

The reasons for this dramatic parenting shift are many and varied. They include a variety of social and health related problems such as, economic hardship, neglect, abandonment, child abuse, teenage pregnancy, substance abuse, incarceration, divorce, domestic violence and HIV/AIDS, among others.

Of course, your role as a grandparent will be subject to family configurations and needs. Perhaps a full-time commitment or a weekend together; an afternoon play date, a summer vacation, a chat on the phone or even an email exchange.

Whatever the specific circumstance, the best grandparenting activities flow naturally from the interests of the grandparents, grandchildren and their own parents. So to ensure a long and successful relationship it is important to get off to a really good start that'll be beneficial to everyone.

Getting Off to a Really Good Start

First of all, if you're called upon to care for your grandchild or grandchildren at the home of your son or daughter, don't expect to be the guest of honor anymore. Welcome instead to the joyous responsibilities of motherhood once again.

It's an opportunity to play; to "fall in love" again, and to appreciate the magic of a developing mind while sharing the things you're passionate about with a new audience; being available to hear about the ideas and activities that excite them; even spoiling them a little without annoying their parents.

As the "crowned" matriarch of your family and family historian you may also use your breadth of experience to add a rich sense of family tradition—and continuity—to a child's life like no one else can.

But in spite of your best intentions, grandparenting brings

with it complications you probably didn't face when you were parenting the first time, including complicated family dynamics that you may need to adjust to. Every time you think you've got a handle on it, there may be another. In short, there may be a lot to start preparing for.

Establishing a few ground rules. From the beginning, be clear about what role you want to have in your grandchild's life and engage your son or daughter—or both—in the process. They can help you learn about the stages the baby/toddler/child is going through, what his or her interests are, and what the "rules of the house" are with regard to appropriate reading/viewing materials, among others.

If this is your first grandchild what should she call you? Some grandparents resist being called grandma or grandpa. Others are quite comfortable with "mom" or "dad." Some have family or ethnic traditions about what they're called. But grandparents are sometimes given the funniest names by their grandchildren for reasons that can be quite mysterious and inexplicable. Perhaps you and they should decide on your new name together. Hope all goes well!

Get organized. Getting anything done well requires some level of organization. Just as keeping your keys, purse and backpack close to the front door will make your morning rush go smoother, so will keeping your grandson's closet tidy which means that he'll now be able to find his baseball glove in a minute instead of an hour. Getting organized also includes managing your time well.

Establishing a Meaningful Relationship with Your Grandchild

With all of the "getting off to a good start" preparedness out of the way, let's look at a number of ways in which you may easily achieve this. They include spending quality time together:

1. **Make an effort to enjoy leisure time** without thinking about a schedule or what's next on the list to be done. Moving at a slower pace than usual can give children a sense that time can be "stretched"—that you don't need to hurry through activities. And, as with adults, it'll allow them space to feel, reflect and express themselves, without feeling rushed.

2. **If there are other grandchildren** involved, on occasions, spend time with each. It will give you an opportunity to bond, without competition.

3. **Get outdoors**—Children love the outdoors. A trip to the park for instance, can be a great jump off point for some wonderful adventures and happy memories. Nature walks and day hikes also provide lots of interesting things to talk about, and water activities can be great fun. You can start these activities when kids are toddlers, and expand them as they get older.

4. **Play some games**—Board and card games provide a unique opportunity to watch kids in action and to see how they operate in their world.

5. **Take a trip**—Sharing your love of a favorite place will help create special memories. Whether it's a day trip to a national park, a weekend in a nearby city OR, a week-long trip to another favorite destination it'll always be remembered as a special journey with grandma or grandpa. Importantly, you may wish to create an album of those special moments.

6. **Share your interests**—Engaging in hobbies and activities that you or your grandchild love can be a great way to spend time together and learn about each other. Activities that you may not even expect your grandchildren to be interested in, such as knitting or gardening. OR, perhaps interest in something they are passionate about such as trading cards or the Harry Potter book series for

instance, in which they may have a special area of knowledge. This may provide an important point of connection for you.

7. **Talk about work**—If you are still employed, a visit to your place of work can add a dimension to your grandchild's perception of you. If you are retired, pictures and stories about what your working days were like may have the same impact.

8. **Communicate family history**—Tell stories about games or trips you shared when their parent (your son or daughter) was young. This is a great way to weave a "tapestry" of shared experiences for the entire family.

9. **Make notes**—When talking, make notes about their interests, pets' names, books they've read, doll's name—anything you can repeat in the next conversation so they know you've been listening.

10. **When you share photographs,** write stories about the people in the pictures. All of these little things communicate your interest and love.

Whatever activities you engage in, allow yourself time to slow down and become really absorbed in each activity. Children respond positively to special attention and care.

What You Shouldn't Do

Having a grandchild is exciting! But while you're eager to help, remember to do nothing that'll diminish your children's roles as parents.

1. **Try not to take over** and do things your way. Follow the parents' rules. Even if you disagree with them, they're the ones who get to set the rules, not you. Bedtime, feeding time, bath time, naptime, toys, clothing—those decisions belong to them. Your babies may have survived well the way they were brought up by you,

but you must try to follow your own kids' wishes. And only offer advice when asked.

2. **If there's a new baby in the family,** avoid hogging. As much as you love your new grandchild, it's important for Mom to bond with him. Your job is to help her to do that in whatever way you can.

3. **Don't play the name game.** This generation's choices are different from yours. When your kids announce they want to name their baby "Banana," or "Orange," your response should be positive. Names come in cycles, so before you think the name they choose is unusual, keep in mind that by the time that child gets to school age, the attendance list may well resemble a vegetable or fruit basket and they'll fit right in. And if it does come down to suggesting a name at all, my best advice is: Don't!

4. **Don't be a Dr. Spock.** Raising kids is just different today. The expertise is different, the books are different. Babies now sleep on their backs rather than their tummies for a good reason. Don't add your own worries to those of the parents.

5. **Giving gifts.** Don't buy before you ask. Make suggestions, if you must, but listen closely and buy only after an agreement has been reached. That way you won't cause any disappointments if they had their hearts set on a different model, or cause hard feelings by giving an older child something his/her parents were withholding for a reason.

What can you do?

You'll need to change your legal relationship, and your first step is to ask the court to help provide legal custody or guardianship. Should you wish to adopt that child, other legal options are also available.

Changing your legal relationship is a big decision which may mean having to prove that those parents are unfit to raise that child, that your new legal relationship will be best for him.

Before you make any decisions, however, be sure to learn about all the legal options available in your state. You may be surprised at how many options there are. A family law attorney can help.

Getting Help through Public Benefit Programs

Raising a child can put a strain on your pocketbook and you may soon need extra money to support your basic needs. Don't use your savings to pay your extra bills. Instead, see if you can get assistance from federal programs. They've been provided to help you. Your grandchild may be able to get Social Security. He or she may be eligible to get money from your state's Temporary Assistance for Needy Families (TANF) program. Your family might qualify for food stamps. Ask the IRS about the Earned Income Tax Credit and the Child Tax Credit. Both programs can give you extra cash at tax time.

In the resources section we've included links to a number of Web sites and telephone numbers that you can call should you need help.

Education

Check with your local school to find out how to enroll your grandchild. Some states won't let you enroll a child unless you have legal custody. In other states, you only need to show that your grandchild lives with you. After he is enrolled, get to know his teacher. Tell her about his current living situation. And be sure to speak up if you think he needs special services to help him do better in school.

Now let's get down to some really serious issues including a few legal ones.

Caring for Your Grandchildren at Your Home

As opposed to taking care of them elsewhere, circumstances may make it necessary for your grandchild or grandchildren to move in with you. And that may be OK. But are you prepared for this? The home you thought was cozy even a few weeks ago may seem too crowded suddenly. Size isn't the only housing problem you may face. If you live in a rented apartment, landlord's rules on how many people can live there may apply and this issue can give you a major headache to begin.

Do you own your own home? If you do, provided that you are at least sixty-two years old, incentive programs such as reverse mortgage (a government-backed program for turning your home equity into cash) can provide you with the cash you need to make your home more comfortable and child friendly. You won't have to sell the house and move out, neither will you be required to make loan payments each month. In fact, you won't have to pay anything back until you sell your home, permanently move out or die.

While reverse mortgage isn't for everyone, it could be just what you need right now. But be sure to learn more about these mortgages before you make any decisions.

Legal Issues and Legal Rights

Having your grandchild live with you may have started out as an informal arrangement, perhaps for a short time. Legally the biological parents were still in charge and you of course, had no legal rights or legal relationship to that child. In the eyes of the law you were simply an "informal" caregiver.

Suddenly, it becomes apparent that he'd be staying with you for much longer but you'll find it hard to raise your own grandchild without some form of legal rights or a formal legal relationship. You may have trouble enrolling him in school or granting permission to a doctor who may need to treat him; you may have trouble getting financial help or you may worry that an unfit parent may come back to take him away.

Your Health

With the added responsibility of raising grandchildren, you must take extra steps to protect your own health. Among other things, take time each day to relax. Get regular checkups and take your prescribed medicines. Ask for help from friends and relatives if you need to. Find a day care provider so you can get a break now and then. And tell your doctors if you feel depressed. They can help.

Your grandchild's health is important too. Even a healthy boy or girl needs regular checkups and immunizations. You may be able to get help from Medicaid or the Children's Health Insurance Program (CHIP). Each state has a CHIP program. CHIP pays for doctor visits, hospital stays, shots and medicines.

Finally, Find a Support Group

A plethora of local support groups and national organizations have sprung up all across the United States. Support groups such as the AARP Grandparent Information Center, Generations United, Grandparents Raising Grandchildren, GAP (Grandparents as Parents), and ROCKing (Raising Our Children's Kids) can help.

In the resource section, we provide a number of Web sites and phone numbers that you can call for assistance.

I know it may feel like ancient history since you were a new mom or dad yourself but so many things about child rearing have changed in the last few years. It is understandable that you may have your own fears. But there are many people out there who understand what you're going through and want to help.

Part VI

Miscellaneous

- Things You Need to Know
- Conclusion
- About the Author
- References
- Resources

Twenty
Things You Need to Know

Education

When Should You Begin Teaching Your Child to Read or When Should You Start Reading to Your Child?

It is never too early to begin teaching your child to read, or at least laying the foundation for early literacy skills. Likewise, it's never too early to read to her.

For a child younger than six months old do not concern yourself with how much she'll understand. A child barely able to sit up won't be able to follow a story. What's important is that she is conditioned to hearing your voice and getting used to being around books.

Some experts even suggest that you create a reading corner at home thus making books readily available and inviting.

There are lots of statistics that show the negative effects of illiteracy. But even without knowing these worrisome statistics we should be aware that reading proficiency is essential to success—not only academically but in life.

Children Learn in Different Ways

Like adults, children have unique learning styles and unique ways of processing information. Some learn visually while others are auditory. Still, others require a sequential approach to learning while others feel constrained by this approach.

There's also the dyslexic who learns at his/her own level and pace. Some of their experiences include difficulties with concentration, perception, memory, verbal skills, abstract reasoning, hand-eye coordination, social adjustment.

To foster or ensure academic success these differences must be identified so that they are given the opportunity to learn in ways harmonious with their unique minds.

Art, Music and Physical Education Teachers

Some schools employ these teachers with special training who'll teach classes once or more per week while the regular classroom teacher helps out, prepares lessons or takes a break.

Reading and Special Education Teachers

Reading teachers are specially trained to help children with learning problems to improve their reading skills. They typically work with an individual child or with a small group of children diagnosing individual problems and providing remedial help.

Special Education teachers are also specially trained to deal with learning problems. Their scope, however, is somewhat broader including writing, math, study skills and other parts of the curriculum.

Teacher Aides

Teacher's aides are often hired to assist teachers in classrooms, to supervise lunches, to work in the school library or to assist in many other ways. Teacher's aides are usually people who are fond of children and who have a lot to offer but who do not have the required license to teach. They can be very important to your child.

Teenage Difficulties

Stress—A Hidden Danger

Being young doesn't necessarily mean being stress free. As adults we tend to view the world of children as happy and carefree. But even very young children have worries and feel stress to some degree. Unfortunately, it often remains a hidden danger in a child's life.

Sources of Childhood Stress

Pressures often come from outside sources (such as family, friends, or school), but they can also come from within.

A two-year-old child, for example, may be anxious because the one person she needs at any given time—a parent—isn't there to satisfy her needs. In preschoolers, separation from parents is the greatest cause of anxiety.

As children get older, academic and social pressures (especially the quest to fit in) also create stress but your child's stress level may be intensified by other factors such as illness, death of a loved one or a divorce.

Recognizing Symptoms of Stress

It isn't always easily recognized. But short-term behavioral changes, such as mood swings, acting out, changes in sleep patterns, or bedwetting, are all indicators. Some children may also experience physical effects, including stomachaches and headaches. Others have trouble concentrating or completing schoolwork. Still others become withdrawn or spend a lot of time alone. Older children may begin to bully, defy authority or display drastic changes in academic performance.

Reducing Your Child's Stress Levels

Proper rest and good nutrition can help. Whether she needs to talk or just be in the same room with you, make yourself available.

Talk with her about what may be the cause. Together, you can come up with a few solutions. Some possibilities are cutting back on after-school activities, spending more time talking with parents or teachers.

You can also help by anticipating potentially stressful situations and preparing her for them.

NOTE: Some level of stress is normal; let your child know that it's OK to feel scared, lonely or anxious. Let her know that other people share those feelings too.

If you are unsuccessful getting to the source of her troubles, however, see her doctor and talk with the counselors and teachers at her school.

Adolescence

Adolescence (children from twelve to nineteen years old) is divided into three stages: early, middle and late adolescence during which time many central themes that most adolescents experience become obvious. During early adolescence they often experience moodiness and a desire to be more independent. That's when friends become extremely important in their lives, when their peer groups will help to define their interests.

In middle adolescence you may notice an even greater desire for independence and autonomy. Among other things, they'll want more privacy and appear to rely less on you. During late adolescence there's greater focus on their future and goals.

Adolescent years can be difficult for both parent and child, a time when you may be tested in many ways. Although being firm and setting limits on many important issues may still be necessary, flexibility counts here. That's when they're trying to find their own identity yes, but it's also a time when they also rely greatly on you.

Anger and Violence

Every year violence claims a staggering number of young lives in the United States.

According to the Center for Disease Control, in the United States, children under fifteen years are murdered at a higher rate than children in any other industrialized nation. The same holds true for suicide. The CDC report cites firearms as the leading cause of these deaths.

According to the said report, "American children are five times more likely to be murdered, two times more likely to kill themselves and twelve times more likely to die from gun fire than children in all the other twenty-five industrial countries combined."

How to Defuse an Angry Child!

1. Do not panic. Listen carefully to any outburst(s) in an attempt to determine the reason(s) or the underlying problem(s) causing such outbursts.
2. Do not retaliate. Never use threats and avoid punishments without understanding the reason for any anger.
3. Let him understand that you—and others—are being hurt. Not in an attempt to cause guilt but in an effort to help him realize how concerned you are for his well being and that of the rest of the family.
4. Re-examine the rules. Perhaps some of the old rules can

be adjusted or changed to new ones that you can both live with.

5. Adjust your own behavior. Anger is often a cry for help. A cry to help them navigate their own twists and turns in life.

No one likes having to deal with an angry child and at times you may even feel that you do not recognize your own child anymore. But a certain amount of teenage anger is inevitable and how you handle such anger could make or break the relationship of not just with one child but with everyone else in the process.

Tax Matters

Earned Income Tax Credit

The Earned Income Tax Credit—or EITC—is for low-income people and families. You don't have to be raising a child to receive this tax credit. But people who are raising children get a bigger tax break.

NOTE: To get the EITC, you must work during the tax year. You must also file a federal tax return. There are age limits for the children you claim. For a full-time student you may claim until he/she turns twenty-four. Children of any age may qualify if disabled.

Do you have at least one child at home? Then you can receive advance payments of the EITC in your weekly paycheck. To receive your credit in advance, you must fill out a W-5 form at work.

Tax Tips for Caregivers Raising Grandchildren

You can claim from the IRS for every child living in your home. If you qualify, you'll undoubtedly pay less to Uncle Sam each year.

Twenty-one
Conclusion

Thanks again for the privilege of being part of your world. Hopefully as a parent many of your kids are still buzzing about you. Perhaps when you bought *Parenting for Tomorrow* in fact, you were on an earnest quest to find that elusive golden key to raising them safely, wisely, with a trifle less commotion and above all, successfully, in these difficult times.

During my very first few weeks on the job, back in 1985, I remember meeting with a number of well-meaning parents, many with the same desires and aspirations, and I made a commitment back then to do everything within my abilities to support those aspirations. I've since tried to keep my word and this book is part of that promise.

It can only take you this far, however. But there are a number of services including government-subsidized programs, set up to assist you regardless of the level of help, guidance or support you'll need.

They do so in complete confidence and I sincerely hope it'll be easy for you to find a good one in your hometown.

If you live in the USA, your local township should be able to advise you on how to find many of those vital services but I've also included a few places of interest in the resource section coming up shortly.

If you live in Brooklyn, by the way, you're also welcome to call our office at 1-718-771-3136.

Finally, of all the benefits you'll enjoy as a parent, none will be as gratifying as seeing your child grow up to become that strong, purposeful citizen that you probably always dreamed of.

Well, starting today, their lives might be about to take on a whole new meaning. But it all begins with you. They'll be with you for a very short period in the span of a lifetime and what you do during their brief stay will determine, to a large extent, what they do with the rest of their lives. . . .

Hopefully you will provide them, therefore, with the right tools to help them cope with life's challenges in their many forms, and with the direction they need so they can carry themselves with kindness, dignity and purpose and grow up to be the caring, focused and successful men and women who'll make us proud.

Happy Parenting!

About the Author

John Samuel, ACSW, LCSW, is a Clinical Social Worker with twenty-one years' experience in the field of social services, here in Brooklyn, New York.

Born in Grenada, West Indies, John obtained his Cambridge Junior Certificate from Cambridge University in England upon leaving primary school. He then worked with the postal services before migrating to England where he obtained his B.Sc. Degree (Honors) as an external student of London University.

John Samuel subsequently taught in secondary education in London before his return to Grenada to join the Civil Service as an Administrative Cadet in the Prime Minister's office in 1968. He later became Personal Assistant to the Governor of Grenada and in 1971 obtained a diploma in International Relations at the University of the West Indies.

In 1973, John became Permanent Secretary in the Ministry of Agriculture and subsequently, Permanent Secretary in the Ministry of Social Affairs, Culture and Community Development.

Diplomatic Service

In 1978 John Samuel became a Grenada Representative to the Organization of American States (OAS) in Washington, D.C.

Social Work Profession

In 1985, John obtained a Master's Degree in Social Work and

two years later became the director of Family Dynamics, Inc., a leading social service agency in New York. And it's out of these experiences that he finally went on to establish his own practice, one that exemplifies his own philosophies regarding children, their development and well-being and family life as a whole.

I first met John at Family Dynamics where I served that agency as consulting psychologist. His rapid advancement there is indicative of his competence, dedication and commitment.

If we measure success by the number of lives we touch and the ways that we reach out to others and truly make a difference, then it's hard to imagine a richer life.

I am, therefore, deeply honored and appreciative that John has asked me to write this brief biography. I'm also proud to have been a member of his Family and Consulting Services Advisory Board from its inception. It is my hope that this presentation of his wisdom and knowledge has been instructive and inspirational for all who've traversed these pages. I encourage every parent to use it and take every suggestion to heart, and not be among those who'd be asking twenty or thirty years from now, Where was *Parenting for Tomorrow* when we were raising our kids?

—Quinton B. Wilkes, Ph.D.
Psychologist/Consultant

116

References

Brenner, Charles, MD. *An Elementary Textbook of Psychoanalysis.* Revised edition, 1974.

Ekman, Paul, Ph.D. *Why Kids Lie—How Parents Can Encourage Truthfulness,* Charles Scribner & Sons, 1989.

Eyre, Linda and Richard. *Teaching Your Children Values,* 1993.

Faber, Adele & Elaine Mazlish. *How to Talk So Kids Will Listen and Listen So Kids Will Talk,* Avon Books, New York, NY, 1982.

Family Therapy Networker, September/October 1999 issue.

Fraiberg, Selma. *The Magic Years—Understanding and Handling the Problems of Early Childhood,* 1959.

Hatchet, Judge Glenda. *Say What You Mean and Mean What You Say,* 2004.

Horthen, Helen. *Clinical Social Work,* New York, Columbia University Press, 1982.

Potter-Efron, Ron. *Angry All the Time—an Emergency Guide to Anger Control,* New Harbinger Publications, Inc., 1994.

Towle, Charlotte. *Common Human Needs*, (1945) Revised edition by NASW, 1987.

Resources

Counseling and Crisis Management

Family and Consulting Service
Tel: 1-718-771-3136

Interfaith Mobile Crisis Team
Tel: 1-718-613-6618

Parent Helpline
Tel: 1-800-342-7472

Big Brother/Big Sister
Tel: 1-212-686-2042

Domestic Violence Helpline
Tel: 1-800-621-4673

N.Y.C. 24-hour Youth Line
Tel: 1-800-246-4646

Education

Dial a Teacher
Tel: 1-212-598-9205

Neighborhood After-School Programs
Tel: 1-212-571-2664

Public Benefit Programs

Free food for seniors and kids—Kings County
Tel: 1-718-498-9208

http://www.benefitscheckup.org

Temporary Assistance For Needy Families (Tanf)

http://www.acf.hhs.gov/programs/ofa/
Or call your local Department of Human Services. Other benefits
may include Social Security. Visit the Social Security Administration (SSA) site at
http://www.ssa.gov. Tel: 1-800-772-1213.

The Food Stamp Program
http://www.fns.usda.gov/fsp
Tel: 1-800-221-5689

**The Special Supplement Food Program For Women, Infants
and Children (WIC)**

Health Services

Center for Mental Health Services
A Federal Government clearinghouse offering mental health Eng-
lish and Spanish language publications for families, children, and
adolescents.
http://www.mentalhealth.org/child
Tel: 1-800-789-2647

National Institute of Mental Health
The mental health research component of the National Institutes of Health, which provides printed and online materials.
http://www.nimh.nih.gov
Tel: 1-301-443-4513

Substance Abuse and Mental Health Services
Administration's Family Guide To Keeping Youth Mentally Healthy & Drug Free.
http://family.samhsa.gov/talk/effects.aspx

Substance Abuse and Mental Health Service
Guide To Keeping Youth Mentally Healthy & Drug Free.
http://family.samhsa.gov/talk/effects.aspx

Federal Center for Mental Health Services
www.mental/health.samhsa.gov/child
Tel: 1-800-789-2647

American Academy of Child & Adolescent Psychiatry
Professional membership organization of psychiatrists provides resources for parents and teens.
http://www.aacap.org
Tel: 1-800-333-7636

Dougy Center, The National Center for Grieving Children and Families
http://www.dougy.org
Tel: 503-775-5683

GriefNet
An Internet community of more than 30 E-mail support groups and two web sites, offering a moderated chat room for children

who are in grief and their parents.
http://www.griefnet.org

Money Management

AARP Resources: *Managing the Money You Earn*
To reach your financial goals, you've got to manage your money—by saving, investing, borrowing wisely, and getting the right advice.

Miscellaneous Resources

State Fact Sheets for Grandparents and Other Relatives Raising Children
http://research.aarp.org/general/kinship_care.html

Fact sheets for each state that provides information about resources and services for grand families.
http://assets.aarp.org/www.aarp.org_/wdi/families/grandparents/public_assistance/foster_care.pdf

Children's Defense Fund: a national child advocacy organization whose mission is to Leave No Child Behind®.
http://www.childrensdefense.org/

Generations United: a national organization that promotes intergenerational strategies, programs, and policies.
http://www.gu.org/

Education, legal support, support groups, and other organizations for grandparents raising grandchildren
http://www.grandparentagain.com/

A free service used by older Americans and their families to identify state and federal assistance programs.
http://www.benefitscheckup.org/